Dealing With Differences

CORWIN
PRESS

The Corwin Press logo—a raven striding across an open book—represents the happy union of courage and learning. We are a professional-level publisher of books and journals for K-12 educators, and we are committed to creating and providing resources that embody these qualities. Corwin's motto is "Success for All Learners."

Dealing With Differences:

Taking Action
On Class, Race, Gender, and Disability

Angele Ellis
and
Marilyn Llewellyn

CORWIN PRESS, INC.
A Sage Publications Company
Thousand Oaks, California

For information address:

Corwin Press, Inc.
A Sage Publications Company
2455 Teller Road
Thousand Oaks, California 91320
E-mail: order@corwin.sagepub.com

SAGE Publications Ltd.
6 Bonhill Street
London EC2A 4PU
United Kingdom

SAGE Publications India Pvt. Ltd.
M-32 Market
Greater Kailash I
New Delhi 110 048 India

Printed in the United States of America

Library of Congress Cataloging-in-Publication Data

Ellis, Angele
        Dealing with differences : taking action on class, race, gender,
and disability / Angele Ellis, Marilyn Llewellyn.
                p.   cm.
        Includes bibliographical references (p.   ).
        ISBN 0-8039-6430-7 (pbk. : acid-free paper)
        1. Prejudices—United States—Problems, exercises, etc.
2. Individual differences—United States—Problems, exercises, etc.
3. Multiculturalism—Study and teaching (Secondary)—United States.
4. Individual differences—Study and teaching (Secondary)—United
States.   I. Llewellyn, Marilyn.   II. Title.
        BF575.P9E38 1996
        305—dc21   96-51300

97 98 99 00 01 02 03 10 9 8 7 6 5 4 3 2

Editorial Assistant:	Kristin L. Green
Production Editor:	Michèle Lingre
Production Assistant:	Karen Wiley
Typesetter/Designer:	Christina Hill
Cover Designer:	Christopher Ellis

Contents

Foreword

I will always remember the first time I saw the authors of this book at work. They had invited me to observe a session of their prejudice and diversity program, which was in its first use in an urban high school. The session was on gender and began with students reviewing a list of toys, checking off which ones they would give to boys, to girls, or to both boys and girls. Within the first five minutes, a student exclaimed that she would never give a doll to a boy because, as her daddy always said, "God made Adam and Eve, not Adam and Steve." The class had careened into antigay fears and stereotypes. Immediately, students began talking with their neighbors, giggling nervously, and the classroom chatter became louder and louder.

Marilyn Llewellyn, an experienced teacher who listens to everything that is said and understands its impact and significance, rallied the attention of the class back to the subject that had been put on the table. She neither avoided it nor responded with empty preaching. Instead, she had the class discuss what had just been proposed and examine how it was—or was not—an example of stereotype and prejudice. Instead of voicing previously stated opinions and going no further, the students in this class began to listen to one another, to question their own positions. I witnessed what the authors stress is one of the aims of this study/action guide: to establish zones of respect (Chapter 1) in which students and teachers can talk about their differences.

How to establish zones of respect in which to talk about differences is one of the most important challenges of civic life. Education is a site where this action must occur. But it is easier said than done. This book differs from other volumes on diversity in education in that it is not solely a collection of thought pieces. Rather, it is a practical guide for teachers and community activists, filled with applications in which thought and practice are integrated. For example, when guidelines for group interaction are agreed on at the beginning of the process (Chapters 1 and 2), zones of respect can be more easily established. Many of us who teach on these issues become inspired by theoretical writings, but have a difficult time figuring out how to make them accessible to and transformative for our students. This volume provides original and creative exercises necessary to continue this work.

Most important, in my opinion, this book does not simplify the problem. The text and exercises are designed to reveal the complex intersection of diversities within each individual and between individuals. The authors do not limit discussions of diversity to gender and race, but interweave the issues of social class and disability, disrupting common associations and turning normal assumptions topsy-turvy. The exercises in this book will awaken teachers to the richness in their own classrooms and help students to get to know one another from different vantage points.

After the class I observed, I listened to Angele Ellis reflect on what had occurred with the regular classroom teacher. In this case, the teacher was a man, who during this session had sat in a row near the back of the classroom, doing paperwork, never looking up. This teacher later had a conversation with Angele in which he told her of his fear and disapproval of the discussion. For adults to teach about prejudice and stereotypes, we ourselves must be able to coexist, to stay in relationship, and to communicate across differences. Adolescents have keen detectors for disingenuity in adults.

Most teachers who initiate diversity-related work want to awaken students to and convince them of alternative points of view. At the same time, we believe in critical thinking. We get caught in a dilemma: How do we genuinely hear differences and elicit critical thinking when we can be said to have our own agendas? What techniques can we use to foster independent thinking? How can we stop ourselves from preaching? As a teacher of gender and language and other hot-button topics, I have found that one of my biggest challenges is not to overlay one ideology on top of another.

Teachers with similar concerns will appreciate "I-search" (Chapter 2), a type of research that stimulates the reader to think about a reading and to ask his or her own questions: What is this reading telling me that I already know and think is important? What is this reading telling me that I don't know and need to know more about? Posing these questions of oneself in all disciplines is a systematic way to help students learn to take ownership of their own thinking, to generate their own ideas. The exercises presented in this volume go way beyond the topic of diversity. They are useful for building an engaged and thinking classroom.

This volume lives and breathes around the goal of the engaged learner. The authors have worked hard to transform the all-too-typical passive experience of reading into one of engaged, active learning. They encourage readers—both teachers and students—to pause throughout the book, reflecting on whether what they have read is best for their own situation.

This excellent volume combines current educational theory with educational practice. It is written by authors who know in their bones that lived experience is part of education, that process is as important as content, and that pedagogy is as important as curriculum. Angele and Marilyn have led lives of community building, reflection, introspection, and contemplation. They have examined their habits of mind (Chapter 1) and have worked at acquiring new ones. They are extremely sensitive to issues of power and inequity, and know that inequities can occur in any setting, regardless of ideology.

Those of us doing work in diversity are fortunate to have this book as a guide. I recommend that teachers use this volume as the authors suggest. Give it the time required, for it will enrich your classroom regardless of what you teach. Take what you think is appropriate, change it, criticize it, and improve it. This is the authors' hope for their book.

Jane Margolis, Ed.D.
Adjunct Assistant Professor
University of Pittsburgh Graduate School of Education
Visiting Research Scientist
Carnegie Mellon University
Computer Science Department

Preface

Education is not preparation for life; education is life itself.

—John Dewey (attributed in Kaplan, 1992, p. 577)

Dealing With Differences: Taking Action on Class, Race, Gender, and Disability is a new kind of book, a *study/action guide* developed from a project on difference and prejudice, Dealing With Prejudice, that we implemented at a Pittsburgh high school for four months in 1994 and evaluated through surveys and in-depth interviews. The book provides a basic introduction to difference and prejudice around issues of class, race, gender, and disability, focused on the complex interconnections among these issues in the context of contemporary U.S. society. Designed primarily as a supplemental program for use in the high school humanities classroom twice a week for a semester or an entire school year, *Dealing With Differences* also has applications as a resource for teachers and students of education and for community groups.

In this book, we erase the traditional distinction between teacher guide and student textbook. *Dealing With Differences* is a comprehensive outline of interactive exercises, discussion topics, and readings, written to be accessible to teachers, administrators, students, and community members committed to working together to address the differences and prejudices they face. Team teaching and strong student participation are integral to implementation of *Dealing With Differences*. Attention to these needs is reflected in both format and content of this book.

At the heart of *Dealing With Differences* is an educative process that relies on the sharing of lived experience, the events that have shaped and continue to shape those present in the classroom. In this process, the sometimes-painful conflicts that arise when differences of race, gender, class, and disability are brought out into the open are used positively, as forces for creation and change. Our educative process is in line with the fifth model of multicultural education defined by Sleeter and Grant (1987), education that is multicultural and social reconstructionist (EMC-SR), promoting social and structural equality and preparing students to work actively for equality in the classroom and community.

The exercises, discussion topics, and readings in *Dealing With Differences* provide a framework for this intense and intensely rewarding process. They are designed to help teachers and students work cooperatively and think critically. Cooperative learning and critical thinking are skills essential to the exploration of how difference is constructed, how prejudice develops around difference, and how difference and prejudice affect people both inside and outside the classroom.

Chapter 1, "Introduction: Exploring the Teachable Moment," discusses the personal, school, and community resources teachers and students must draw on to implement *Dealing With Differences* successfully. In this chapter, we refer to our own teaching and learning experience, including our experience with our pilot program Dealing With Prejudice, to illuminate the importance of these resources for our readers.

Chapter 2, "Beginning the Process," shifts the action to the classroom. We start by encouraging participants to know and trust one another, asking them to engage in a number of interactive exercises and to develop guidelines for classroom interaction. The chapter also familiarizes participants with the basics of critical thinking and cooperative learning. The format of exercises, discussion topics, and readings introduced in Chapter 2 is continued and expanded on in Chapters 3 through 7.

Each of the next four chapters—Chapter 3, "Class and Classism"; Chapter 4, "Race, Racism, and Xenophobia"; Chapter 5, "Gender, Sexism, and Heterosexism"; and Chapter 6, "Disability and Ableism"—concentrates on one major area of difference and prejudice. At the same time, each encourages participants to explore the ways in which these differences and prejudices are related. Participants may raise issues not specifically addressed in *Dealing With Differences*—such as age and ageism—while using these chapters.

Dealing With Differences introduces class first because social and economic differences are often ignored or minimized in U.S. society and because constructs of class and classism have influenced constructs of race, gender, and disability. Race and gender—hot-button issues that provoke fears of conflict—are introduced next, after participants are comfortable with the process. Race is placed before gender because the consciousness of race and racism has influenced the development of consciousness of gender, sexism, and heterosexism. Disability is introduced last because it has been a hidden issue, one just beginning to be recognized as a source of struggle for rights and identity.

Chapters 3 to 6 are designed to be used in sequence, building on and flowing into one another. Participants have the option, however, of using one or more of these chapters separately after they have completed Chapter 2.

Chapter 7, "Continuing the Commitment," like Chapter 2 is essential to the process of this book. Chapter 7 provides participants with a period of reflection and discussion after they have finished the other chapters. It includes a closing ceremony designed to bring participants together and to give them something tangible by which to remember the program.

"You have to teach the different hatreds, so then you can teach how to stop them," one of our students said in an interview after our pilot program Dealing With Prejudice. "Some people don't know really what ageism or sexism is. They think it's just like old people versus young people, and men versus women, when it can be women versus women, and old people versus old people. You have to teach that, and then we can find a way to stop it."

Angele Ellis
Marilyn Llewellyn
Pittsburgh, Pennsylvania

Acknowledgments

Producing a book, like teaching, requires intense collaboration and commitment. Throughout this project's four-year cycle—developing an experimental high school pilot project on contemporary issues of difference and prejudice, implementing it in five ninth-grade classrooms for 16 weeks, evaluating its impact through 150 surveys and 30 in-depth interviews, and revising it into the proposal and manuscript of *Dealing With Differences*—we have learned and benefited from the efforts of many people.

We thank the following individuals: Delores Avner, Margaret Berry, Jamila Bey, Bill Bigelow, Mary Elizabeth Brush, Roberta Campbell, Shelly Casey, Amanda Clark, Mary Susan Connell, Roshawn Cooper, Judith Ann Criner, Mary Margaret Doorley, Bob Douds, Rose Duhon-Sells, Shana Eberhardt, Tiffany Eberhardt, Jim Faltot, Elena Featherston, Rhodora Freyvogel, Noreen Garman, Maureen Haggarty, Nelson Haggerson, Leigh-Anne Halama, Mary Hamler, MeShelda Jackson, Anna Katselas, Michelle Keffer, Sandy Kiefer, Mimi Koumanelis, Anne Kuhn, Claudette Kulkarni, Bettina Lee, Cheryl Massimo, Lynn Miller, Reggie Miller, Janet Montelaro, Basilio Montiero, Jen Moriarty, Bridgette Morton, Sara Moss, Marianne Novy, Barney Oursler, L. Jalik Petty, Maria Piantanida, Beth Pluto, Linda Schoyer, Janet Seltman, Charles Shealey, Adrien Sirolli, Millie Skovran, Lucy Spruill, Micheline Stabile, Karen Stanfield, Ann Strosser, Erin Timblin, Vince Tucker, Cassandra White, Iris Young, and the 150 ninth-grade students who participated in the first use of these materials, especially those whose words are quoted (with permission) in this book.

Special thanks to Elizabeth Brown, Jeanette Bussen, Cynthia Comiskey, Anna Marie Gaglia, Dolores Montini, and Patricia Phillips; Christopher Ellis, Alice Foster, and the staff of Corwin Press; Adeline Llewellyn, Jane Margolis, Veronica Morgan-Lee, and Mark Murphy.

We are indebted to the Maurice Falk Medical Fund for its generous support of both our high school pilot project and this book. Our thanks to staff member Darla Grzybowski and board members Philip Baskin, Bertram Brown, Estelle Comay, Sigo Falk, Julian Ruslander, and Eric Springer.

Our deepest gratitude to Phil Hallen, president of the Maurice Falk Medical Fund, for his dedication to the work.

About the Authors

Angele Ellis is a writer and community organizer who has worked in alternative education for 12 years, developing programs and creating learning partnerships for adult and adolescent learners on issues of race, gender, culture, and nonviolence. She is a former codirector of the Pittsburgh Peace Institute, which in 1993 nominated her for the *Pittsburgh Post-Gazette* Pittsburgher of the Year Award for a series of high school seminars on the Columbus quincentennial. She earned a B.A. in English from the University of Pittsburgh. She also has worked as a technical and business writer and a freelance writer and editor.

Marilyn Llewellyn has been an education professional for over 20 years, working as a teacher and administrator at the elementary and secondary school levels. For 10 years, she taught high school history, English, religion, and drama, encouraging students to learn about social responsibility and the creation of a society where difference is respected. Her teaching awards include the 1990 Great Teacher Recognition Award, the 1992 Golden Apple Award, and the 1992 Thanks to Teachers Award. She earned a B.A. in history and secondary education from Carlow College and an M.A. in American and early modern European history from Boston College, and is completing a self-designed Ph.D. in education curriculum and instructional design from The Union Institute.

1

Introduction: Exploring the Teachable Moment

When I first started teaching, I didn't know what to expect. After sitting in enough classes, I began to put my feelings on different issues into my teaching. I found that a lot of freshmen understood what I was saying and that felt good. We learned a lot about each other that way.

—high school senior and student teacher from pilot program Dealing With Prejudice

Dealing With Differences was born in October 1992, in a moment of great crisis and greater opportunity. A group of 75 juniors from an urban high school, nodding though a three-hour program on American Indian culture organized by one of the authors of this book, became electrified when the program speaker threw out this question: "As an American Indian, I am offended by sports teams with names like the Cleveland Indians and Atlanta Braves. What do you think?"

1

What happened next, in the words of the teacher who accompanied her students to the program:

> What a memorable day!!! In less than two hours these women were able to unleash all of the prejudice that we brought with us. The Afro-American and Asian students were shocked at the insensitivity of the White students in regard to the Indians. There were impassioned exchanges and even tears shed in that assembly.

This teachable moment did not end with the tears and passions that for a few tense hours had seemed to shatter fragile psyches and relationships. The students "never stopped talking about the program," according to their teacher, who gave them the support necessary to continue to explore their deep-seated attitudes about race and to work toward constructive change:

> From October 17 to June 10, we were engaged in many projects and discussions on how to eradicate racism. We went to see *Malcolm X* and viewed two of Oprah Winfrey's after-school specials on teens and racism. The movie and videos were followed by discussion. By April, we were speaking and listening to one another with respect and acceptance. I'd say it was an 85% improvement in communication since October 16.

Excited by these developments, with the teacher's help the two of us began to plan an expanded program on prejudice and difference for implementation in this school. For this pilot program, Dealing With Prejudice, we constructed a framework to help students explore the connections between race and other issues, including gender and class.

In September 1993, as Dealing With Prejudice was being written and organized for use in one classroom, crisis and opportunity struck again. Several African-American first-year students at the school received hate notes in their lockers, notes that contained racial slurs and threatened the students with violence if they did not leave the school.

Some of the students who had attended the October 1992 program had formed an after-school group called Students in Search Of. . . . They now stepped in to confront the hatred and violence. They asked for and received permission from the school administration to hold a special assembly in which they spoke of the pain of their own experiences with racism and their belief that racist violence should not be tolerated in their school. Although the senders of the notes were never identified, no more notes were received.

School administrators, both shaken and impressed by these events, asked us to expand the developing program to include all 150 first-year students. Realizing that we could not and did not want to attempt this task alone, we recruited 20 individuals to work in teaching teams, giving us three to five teachers for each of the five classes of first-year students. These teaching teams were both inter-racial and intergenerational. Drawing on resources from the school community and the local community, they included teachers, counselors, social workers, psychologists, community organizers, and students. Nine team members were high school seniors involved in Students in Search Of . . . Community concern about the racist notes made it easier to involve a larger and more diverse group of teachers in the project, another instance of crisis leading to opportunity.

For 16 weeks in February to May 1994, these teaching teams went into classrooms once a week to engage students on questions of race, gender, class, and other issues. We participated in, observed, and took notes on each of the 80 sessions. Anxiety over coping with the crises that continued inevitably to arise was balanced by the opportunity to observe students growing in confidence, cooperation, critical thinking, and compassion. We were astonished and humbled by the depth of the insights expressed by students once they became involved in a program committed to giving them a basis for thinking, speaking, and acting for themselves.

When some students in one class became angry and unresponsive after teachers introduced the notion that the terms *angel food cake* and *devil's food cake* had racist implications, we stopped the class entirely to devote an entire session to the expression of students' feelings. The look of excitement on one student's face when she realized that she could vent her criticisms without fear of being silenced or punished freed all of the participants to go on exploring race with more understanding than before.

When during discussions of homophobia some students made homophobic remarks and some adult teachers became uncertain and nervous about addressing the issue, it was the senior student teachers who responded with honesty and sensitivity, "putting their own feelings into the teaching." One senior student's acknowledgment of her mother's lesbianism and another's affirmation of her gay friends helped participants to begin to question stereotypes about sexuality.

When the students gave Dealing With Prejudice low marks in a survey distributed at the program's midpoint, telling us that it was not fulfilling its promise to allow them to deal with prejudice, we reinterpreted the written materials we had prepared so carefully to concentrate on the contemporary issues of prejudice and difference that students wanted to talk and learn about. These issues were rooted in relationships with family, friends, neighbors, teachers, and classmates. As in the three-hour program that sparked Dealing With Prejudice, approaching the political through the personal turned something dull and remote into something vivid and immediate for most students.

Starting from this point, the students made sharper and deeper connections between their own lived experience and the constructs and "isms" raised by the program materials. The students elaborated on these connections in their final surveys and in the 30 in-depth interviews we conducted with selected students and teachers during the six months after the Dealing With Prejudice pilot program ended. Student ideas on both process and content—some of which are quoted in this book—were a major influence in determining the scope and structure of our revised and expanded program for this book.

By the end of the pilot program, the students gave it an approval rating of over 80%; more than 50% of the students rated it as 4 or 5 on a 1-to-5 scale. When asked on their final surveys if the program should continue at their school, some students made the following comments:

> Yes, because prejudice exists in the world and we should know ways to help prevent it and to help people become more aware.

> Yes, it was insightful and thought provoking, and I believe that it would help to make our school a better place.

> Yes, because not everyone knows the power of prejudice and the hurt.

Necessary Resources

We began this chapter with a brief history of the crises and opportunities of the pilot program that led to the development of *Dealing With Differences* because we realize that dealing with the power of prejudice and the hurt is a daunting process, both inside and outside the classroom. Readers may well be asking themselves, So now what? How can I introduce this program into my school or community group? What do I need to make it happen? What do I need to make it really work?

The following list of necessary resources, arranged alphabetically, includes both resources used in the original Dealing With Prejudice pilot program and resources added and refined during the evaluation process that followed this implementation, based on our field notes and on participant surveys and interviews. We urge readers seriously interested in implementing *Dealing With Differences* to study and discuss this list with their colleagues prior to any use of this program.

Action. "You told us we were going to deal with prejudice, but we never get to the dealing," some of our students complained during the Dealing With Prejudice pilot program. To fulfill this promise, implementation of *Dealing With Differences* must provide students with opportunities for action. This includes not only taking responsibility for classroom exercises and discussions, but initiating projects outside the classroom. There are a number of places in this text where students are encouraged to develop suggestions for action on race, gender, class, and disability issues. These actions can be implemented with the help of teachers, administrators, and community members.

Some of the actions taken by students who participated in the Dealing With Prejudice pilot program—before, during, and after the program—included forming an after-school group on issues of race and racism; running for student government offices on a platform of bringing students together as a community; performing volunteer work with local organizations, including those that deal with hunger and those that deal with violence against women; preparing a school assembly on racism; writing and performing a play on date rape; and conducting a racism awareness day in which students distributed multicolored cookies and signs saying, "It's not a black thing, it's not a white thing, it's not a yellow thing, it's not a red thing, it's not a brown thing, it's a human thing."

Administrative Support. The backing of a high school principal, vice principals, and other administrators was crucial to Dealing With Prejudice. These administrators attended planning and evaluation meetings, sent a letter to parents explaining the program, and sat in on several classes. When issues spilled beyond the boundaries of our classrooms—a student confiding her grief over a friend's suicide, a student mentioning something relevant she was reading in another class—we wished that we had extended our circle of support to counselors and teachers not directly involved in the curriculum. One teacher told us after the program ended that her colleagues in the school's English department had been intrigued by the program and would have liked to discuss topics raised during Dealing With Prejudice in their own classrooms.

Caring. Caring is a fundamental resource, one that can make any curriculum—traditional or alternative—meaningful to students. Many of our students told poignant stories of having been wounded by uncaring teachers and encouraged by caring ones throughout their educational lives. "It could be more than just like, 'I'm teaching you.' Like teachers offering, helping things, and letting students know you care about them," one student said in her post-program interview. "The teachers who care, it's just a whole different attitude in class."

Class Size. Deborah Meier (1995) asserts that a mediocre teacher can accomplish things with 20 students that a brilliant teacher can't accomplish with 40. Our Dealing With Prejudice classes ranged from 22 to 35 students, a difference that seemed more like 22 to

50. In the larger classes, both students and teachers expressed frustration at their inability to be heard in group discussion. One team of teachers decided to take half the class into an empty classroom for the remainder of the program. Other solutions were to rearrange the desks in the classroom into a semicircle and to spend more time in small group discussions.

Community Support. As mentioned, many of our Dealing With Prejudice teachers were drawn from the local community, including a college administrator, a church administrator, a social worker, a psychologist, and two college students involved in their university's cultural diversity group. The presence of these individuals in the classroom impressed students, a few of whom told us in post-program interviews that they wished that their parents had been invited to teach. Scheduling did not permit community teachers to be part of every class, but their presence enriched the program.

Conflict. Conflict often is considered a problem, not a resource, although it is in conflict that growth and change take place. As previously mentioned, our pilot program Dealing With Prejudice was forged in conflict—a passionate and tearful discussion of race and racism in a multiracial class of high school juniors. The program continued to grow as these students grew, initiating projects and discussions on racism, including a student-led assembly to confront the pain of racism after some of their African-American classmates had received hate notes in school. It was the courage and initiative of these students that convinced school administrators to support the Dealing With Prejudice pilot program.

Our experience is that conflict must be addressed. If the guidelines for interaction that participants develop at the beginning of the program are not sufficient to do this, other methods can be employed.

One method for handling conflict, suggested by one of our students, is to place in the classroom a comment box in which participants can place unresolved concerns. The comments in the box can be signed or anonymous. Periodically—once or twice a week—this comment box is emptied and its contents read aloud and discussed in class.

Detracking. One of our students devoted a large part of her post-program interview to a critique of tracking. She told us that the students in lower-track classes in her school—including her best friend—were deprived of opportunities to learn skills such as writing research papers and because of this would "never catch up." Tracking is a serious class and race issue. We urge teachers and administrators to use *Dealing With Differences* as part of their effort to create heterogeneous, untracked classrooms. As Jeannie Oakes (1985) asserts, heterogeneous groups of students can greatly enhance their classroom skills when they become engaged in materials based on real-life experiences and rich with meaning. Even in tracked classes, emphasis on lived experience, critical thinking, and cooperative learning can improve the educational experience for many students.

Diversity. One of the reasons we invited community members and students to teach in the Dealing With Prejudice pilot program was that we did not want to present a program on diversity and prejudice without the help of both men and women, both young people and older people, both white people and people of color. An African-American student told us afterward that she had never before had an African-American teacher and had relished the experience of seeing an African-American in front of the class. One of our African-American teachers, a counselor in a special school district program, told us that she felt closer to her white students by the time the program ended than she had before.

Flexibility. When students became particularly engaged by a discussion or an exercise, we encouraged teachers to take it to its natural conclusion, even if that meant that they skipped other parts of the written curriculum. When students became bored by a discussion or exercise, we encouraged teachers to ask students directly why they were not engaged in the material and to make necessary adjustments. Students whose teachers responded to the need for flexibility complained far less about irrelevance and irritation in their post-program interviews than did students whose teachers doggedly covered every written word.

Grading. Our students needed reassurance that they would not be graded on the opinions they expressed in class—evidence of a fear that exposes how punitive some students find traditional methods of evaluation. Teachers need to develop new and clearly expressed ways of grading this program. We recommend that students be evaluated on participation—their willingness to engage in the process. Some of the exercises included in this book may, in addition, become part of student portfolios.

Guest Speakers. Our students responded positively to two guest speakers from a local group called the Coalition to Counter Hate Crimes. One of the speakers was a 13-year-old boy who conversed with students about what teenagers could do to oppose hate activities. Several students asked for more guest speakers in their surveys and post-program interviews. Chapters 3 to 6 contain exercises in which participants invite into the classroom speakers who have lived experience with class, race, gender, and disability.

Guidelines for Interaction. Every one of our classes developed and posted its own guidelines for interaction—such as "one person talks at a time"—using as a reference a list we provided (see Chapter 2). In the classes where students took an active role in developing their own guidelines in their own words—rather than merely copying the guidelines provided—students respected the rules and reminded each other to follow them when discussions became heated. "When you did that list of goals . . . that kind of made everyone feel they could talk. . . . I personally felt more comfortable speaking out in the class because I knew I had the same rights as everyone else," one student said of the guidelines in her post-program interview.

Habits of Mind. Melinda Fine (1995) calls "democratic habits of mind" (p. 5) the attitudes that make good citizens. Fine asserts that school is the key institution where students learn new habits of mind about dealing with differences. In our experience, students cannot develop new habits of mind unless teachers examine their own attitudes about democracy, including the potential democracy of the classroom. We observed the high school seniors who taught in the Dealing With Prejudice pilot program modeling their attitudes toward students after those of their adult colleagues—open in some cases, closed in others. Habits of mind are powerful forces for both reaction and change. Only by examining their habits of mind on every issue raised in this book—teaching, learning, class, race, gender, and disability—can teachers hope to influence students in the ways that Fine envisions.

Historical Context. Dealing With Differences addresses class, race, gender, and disability within the context of contemporary U.S. society. We encourage history and English teachers and students to enrich the program by incorporating resources and readings from regular curricula and other sources. The evidence participants gather on contemporary concerns through I-search and critical thinking (Chapter 2) can certainly include these historical materials.

Lived Experience. Earlier in this chapter, we described how *Dealing With Differences* was born and grew in moments when participants spoke and acted from lived experience, the complex events that make individuals who they are. It is vital that in using *Dealing With Differences,* emphasis remains not on the text itself but on the generative themes evoked by the text, themes that arise from students' own experiences (Shor, 1992). Participants need to welcome and embrace lived experience, not dismiss it as irrelevant or avoid it as too controversial.

Like a genie in a bottle, lived experience is powerful and frightening—and magical. It is only when lived experience is let out into the classroom that learning becomes real, that what happens on the page or the chalkboard connects to what happens and has happened in the minds, hearts, and bodies of people in the class-room.

Materials. That we had limited copies of the draft curriculum used during Dealing With Prejudice caused both frustration and suspicion among students. "How are we supposed to know what it's about when we can't see it?" one student complained in class. In this text, we attempt to erase the distinction between privileged teacher materials and student materials. *Dealing With Differences* is designed to be shared by all participants. We urge teachers to make it readily available in classrooms and school libraries.

Readings and Videos. One of our students said that in reading works by authors with whom she could identify she was better able to reflect on her own experiences. The readings reprinted in *Dealing With Differences* were chosen because they deal directly with the experiences of young people on class, race, gender, and disability. Most are short enough to be read aloud, a practice that may help to minimize differences in reading skill levels among students. We encourage teachers and students to incorporate books, periodicals, and videos from the resource list provided at the end of the book into the program.

Reflection. The moments of intensity that will occur in this program need to be balanced by moments of reflection. Readings and re-sponses to readings are places where reflection can occur. Another suggestion made by one of our students is to conclude intense classes with five minutes of quiet time, dimming the lights and playing soothing music.

Student Leadership. An essential aspect of *Dealing With Differences* is that all students be given opportunities for leadership, both as teachers and as leaders of individual exercises and discussions. During the Dealing With Prejudice pilot program, we observed student teachers—some of whom had never been considered leaders because they were not star students, athletes, or student officers—become increasingly thoughtful, articulate, and confident. "I was proud of myself, because I felt like a mentor to those students," one student teacher wrote to us after the program ended. The students they were teaching responded well to their slightly older peers. "Whenever she talked, I listened," a student remarked in a post-program interview. The younger students also demanded their own leadership opportunities. "MORE STUDENT-LED DISCUSSIONS!" read a typical request on an evaluation form distributed in Week 8 of our program.

Team Teaching. Team teaching models cooperation, democracy, and diversity for both students and teachers. It shifts learning from passive to active without diminishing teacher responsibility for what happens in the classroom. We became so accustomed to team teaching during the Dealing With Prejudice pilot program that a single teacher in front of the classroom—as happened on a few occasions when other team members had scheduling conflicts—was a lonely sight. Our major difficulty with team teaching was that a tight implementation schedule did not give teachers adequate time to meet to review materials, to plan lessons, or even to chat. This drawback could be remedied by scheduling pre-program meetings in which teaching teams become thoroughly familiar with *Dealing With Differences* and each other, as well as by scheduling regular meetings once the program has begun.

Time. During the Dealing With Prejudice pilot program, time problems affected both teacher preparation and classroom implementation. We were given what seemed like an extravagant amount of time for this type of program, 16 sessions over 16 weeks. We soon realized that it was grossly inadequate. A once-a-week schedule made it nearly impossible for teachers and students to maintain continuity between discussions. Every 40-minute class period left someone or something hanging; we received many complaints about this from both students and teachers. Teachers expressed more and more anxiety about being able to cover the materials, resulting in some of them plowing through lessons rather than allowing them to develop naturally. Because of this experience, we recommend that *Dealing With Differences* be taught at least twice a week, whether it is implemented for a semester or a year. "Just like music or art," one student suggested in a post-program interview. Another student suggested that the program be taught five days a week, an option that is certainly open to those willing to make the commitment.

We are aware that the demands of regular humanities classes may not permit teachers and students to use this book as we—or they—would like. The book is organized to accommodate a variety of options, in the hope that the more teachers and students use it, the more they will want to use it.

Zones of Respect. Respect is the basis of rewarding human relationships. We define zones of respect as spaces in which individuals can deal with their differences honestly, without using or abusing one another. These places can be physical, such a classroom, church, or community center. They can be mental and emotional, such as an assembly or meeting in which individuals agree to confront their differences without violence and with regard for one another's ideas and feelings. Zones of respect can be created among classmates, among neighbors, among family members, among friends, even among former enemies.

Teachers and students established zones of respect during the Dealing With Prejudice pilot program. "This class was different because it gave everybody a chance to talk," one student said in her postprogram interview. "I mean, there were so many different issues that we discussed, and it just let you know people a lot more. . . . Some of the stuff was surprising, that's why I liked it, because you got to learn a lot about people."

Structure of This Book

Deborah Byrnes (1988) asserts that teachers can reduce prejudice among students in their classrooms by engaging in four different kinds of activities: activities that promote positive interactions with those different from oneself on the basis of equality; activities that promote individual self-esteem; activities that encourage the identification of overgeneralizations and stereotypes; and activities that increase empathy and understanding of individuals who are different from oneself. The remaining chapters of *Dealing With Differences* are structured around these four kinds of activities, in a format designed to bring participants to ever deeper levels of understanding of the issues raised in the text. Chapters 3 to 6, which cover class, race, gender, and disability, are nearly identical in format. Chapters 2 and 7, which bracket the issue-oriented chapters with information necessary to begin and end the program, are slightly different in variety of topics and exercises but not in essentials.

The basic chapter format is as follows:

Icebreaker. Each chapter begins with an icebreaker, a creative exercise that introduces the major theme of the chapter while giving participants the opportunity to have fun and get to know one another better.

What Is _____? Each chapter continues with a definition and explanation of its central theme. Every time a chapter theme or subtheme is introduced, it is followed by questions to stimulate reflection and discussion among participants. Discussion questions focus on looking at themes through the lived experience of participants. The questions are deliberately general so as not to lead or limit responses.

Large Group Exercise: DIFFERENCE and VALUE. The ways in which community, class, race, gender, and disability are constructed are examined through word exercises in which participants link the differences they perceive to the values they associate with those differences.

Subtheme. Various subthemes (one of the "isms" in Chapters 3 to 6; communication in Chapter 2) are introduced along with questions for reflection and large group discussion.

Individual Exercise: Media Images. The ways in which class, race, gender, and disability are interpreted in the mass media (television, films, books, magazines, newspapers, music) are explored in an exercise that asks participants to look critically at media images in light of both their own experience and what has been discussed in the program.

Large Group Exercise: Common Ground. Participants come together in Common Ground, an exercise designed to elicit concerns about prejudices or problems around an issue. Common Ground not only brings participants closer but serves as a first step for taking action on their concerns.

Small Group Exercise: Concerns and Suggestions for Action. When participants are first divided into small groups in Chapter 2, the purpose is to deepen their understanding of who they are and the influences that have helped to shape them. When the small groups meet again in subsequent chapters, the purpose is to develop suggestions for action based on the concerns raised during Common Ground. Small group exercises provide participants with opportunities for detailed discussion and research.

Large Group Exercise: Concerns and Suggestions for Action. The concerns and suggestions for action developed in the small groups are shared and refined in this large group exercise. At this point, teachers need to provide students with practical encouragement and assistance on the strongest suggestions for action.

Guest Speaker. The guest speakers mentioned earlier in this chapter are invited into the classroom only after participants have had a chance to explore issues in depth. Guest speakers, like teachers, also may provide students with encouragement and assistance on suggestions for action.

Individual Exercise: Reading and Reflection. The process of reflection, of bringing one's lived experience to a reading, is introduced in Chapter 2. Each chapter ends with a reading (some chapters contain more than one reading) that addresses the themes and subthemes of the chapter from the perspective of an individual speaker or speakers. This exercise encourages participants to put their own ideas and thoughts about the reading into reflections that demonstrate their individual gifts of expression.

2

Beginning the Process

Games would help people to know each other better . . . have little games, but don't pick like friends always to be together. Let them be with someone else that they don't know and like . . . start the class off with games . . . make it a fun class. Then when you start the learning part . . . they'll be knowing each other, and they won't mind sharing their feelings.

—student from pilot program Dealing With Prejudice

Beginning the process is the most important part of Dealing With Differences. *As teachers and students get to know themselves, each other, and the resources available to them—both individual and collective—they will better understand their similarities as well as their differences. Self-knowledge and knowledge of others are essential to building a community within the classroom where participants can explore the complex and interrelated issues of class, gender, race, and disability.*

This chapter introduces the interactive exercises, discussion topics, and readings continued in Chapters 3 to 7. It also examines the concepts of community, cross-cultural (or intercultural) communication, cooperative learning, critical thinking, I-search, multiple intelligences, and reflection. Near the end of this chapter, participants will develop the guidelines for classroom interaction that will shape their discussions and actions throughout the program.

This chapter contains the following sections. The times given to complete them are approximate.

Icebreaker: "Who Am I?" (one to two class sessions)
What Is Community? (one class session)
Large Group Exercise: "What Are My Communities?" (one class session)
Cross-Cultural Communication (two class sessions)
Cooperative Learning (one to two class sessions)
Small Group Exercise: Communication, Culture, and Identity (two class sessions)
Critical Thinking and I-Search (two class sessions)
Large Group Exercise: Critical Thinking and I-Search in Action (two class sessions)
Multiple Intelligences (one class session)
Large Group Exercise: "Who Do I Know Who . . . ?" (one class session)
Guidelines for Interaction in the Classroom (one class session)
Large Group Exercise: Developing Guidelines for Interaction (one class session)
Reflection (one class session)
Individual Exercise: Reading and Reflection—"Ending Poem" (two class sessions)

Icebreaker: "Who Am I?"

Approximate time: one to two class sessions

Icebreakers are large group exercises designed to introduce issues in a way that engages people and allows them to get to know one another better. So many students who participated in our pilot program Dealing With Prejudice requested icebreakers that we decided to begin each chapter with a different one. "Who Am I?" is a simple name-tag icebreaker that nonetheless can reveal surprising similarities and differences. Like all exercises in *Dealing With Differences*, it depends on the participants being respectful of each other and assuming responsibility for the process.

SUPPLIES: One large pin-on name tag for each student and teacher; marking pens; chalkboard and chalk or poster paper.
STUDENT LEADERSHIP: At least two students volunteer to help pass out name tags and marking pens, give instructions for the

exercise, and record discussion results on the chalkboard or on poster paper.

To Begin: The exercise leaders give each participant—teachers as well as students—a name tag and ask that he or she do the following:

1. Write his or her name in the center of the name tag.

2. Write where he or she was born in the upper left-hand corner of the name tag.

3. Write whether he or she is an oldest child, a middle child, a youngest child, or an only child in the upper right-hand corner of the name tag.

4. Write his or her favorite musical performer in the lower left-hand corner of the name tag.

5. Write his or her favorite food in the lower right-hand corner of the name tag.

A completed name tag looks like the one in Figure 2.1.

Figure 2.1. Name Tag

The exercise leaders then ask the participants to put their name tags on and to move their desks to create an open space in the middle of the classroom. The participants group and regroup themselves based on their responses to the following questions from the exercise leaders, who also join in the exercise. At the completion of the exercise, participants return to their seats for large group discussion.

EXERCISE QUESTIONS

1. Everyone born in _____ (ask participants to call out names) move to the front of the classroom, the back of the classroom, the left side, right side, middle, and so on. Say hello and chat for a few minutes.

2. Everyone who is an oldest child move to the back of the classroom. Everyone who is a youngest child move to the front of the classroom. Everyone who is a middle child move to the left of the classroom. Everyone who is an only child move to the right of the classroom. Say hello and chat for a few minutes.

3. Everyone whose favorite musical performer is _____ (ask for names) move to the front of the classroom, the back of the classroom, left side, right side, center, and so on. Say hello and chat for a few minutes.

4. Everyone whose favorite food is _____ (ask for names) move to the front of the classroom, the back of the classroom, left side, right side, middle, and so on. Say hello and chat for a few minutes.

QUESTIONS FOR REFLECTION AND LARGE GROUP DISCUSSION

■ In what ways am I similar to other participants?

■ In what ways am I different from other participants?

■ What surprised me about this exercise?

What Is Community?

Approximate time: one class session

A *community* (from the Latin word *communitas*) is a group of people who live in the same place or share something in common. Communities organized around place can include neighborhoods, cities, states, and countries. They can also include work sites, churches, and schools.

Communities organized around other things that individuals have in common can take a variety of forms. Family is a basic form of community. Friendship is a form of community that for many individuals is as deeply important as family. Communities can be organized around issues of identity—religion, racial or ethnic group, gender, sexual orientation, disability. They can be organized around the sharing of political or social ideas.

Common interests and activities can draw individuals into community. Music, sports, drama, art, and science are points of community. These communities can be highly organized, as in sports teams or after-school clubs, or they can be loosely organized, as in groups of friends who listen to similar music and wear similar clothes.

An individual can belong to several different communities at the same time. These communities can overlap, as when two people become friends who live in the same neighborhood and are part of the same family. These communities can come into conflict, as when two people become friends who live in very different neighborhoods and come from very different families.

Large Group Exercise: "What Are My Communities?"

Approximate time: one class session

In the "What Are My Communities?" exercise, participants list and discuss the various communities to which they belong. These communities can be both general ("my family") and specific ("the Center High Drama Club").

SUPPLIES: Chalkboard and chalk or poster paper and marking pens.

STUDENT LEADERSHIP: At least two students volunteer to help lead large group discussion and record responses on the chalkboard or poster paper.

TO BEGIN: The participants think of and share their membership in as many communities as they can name. The exercise continues until every participant has had the opportunity to speak, although every participant need not speak.

QUESTIONS FOR REFLECTION AND LARGE GROUP DISCUSSION

- What are my communities?
- Which of my communities overlap with one another? Which of my communities are separate from one another?
- Which of my communities do I share with other participants?
- Which of my communities are different from those of other participants?
- What surprised me about this exercise?

Cross-Cultural Communication

Approximate time: two class sessions

Community is rooted in *culture*—the distinctive customs, ideas, and language of a particular group. Every community has its own culture. Individuals who remain in one community learn and adopt one cultural style. Individuals who move among different communities may learn and adopt several cultural styles, which can be strikingly different from one another.

Differences in culture and cultural styles can make it difficult for individuals to understand one another. To create a community in the classroom, individuals need to communicate across and between cultures, a process called *cross-cultural communication* (Taylor, 1987) and, more recently, *intercultural communication* (Eilers, 1993).

Orlando Taylor (1987) offers the following suggestions on effective cross-cultural communication:

1. Be aware of statements that may reflect a prejudgment about an individual or group ("Women are always so emotional," to give one example).

2. Be aware of identifying an individual unnecessarily by his or her membership in a group ("We hired a young black woman"; "He's a very nice Korean student"; "That old white guy said"; "Then, this lady in a wheelchair came in").

3. Be aware of words or phrases that may negatively judge a group ("culturally deprived," "culturally disadvantaged").

4. Be aware that the different ways in which individuals react to silence, loud voices, quiet voices, teasing, slang, and eye contact may be cultural.

5. Be aware of common words and phrases that may refer negatively to individuals or groups ("black as sin," "Indian giver").

6. Be aware that communication is a skill that must constantly be developed.

QUESTIONS FOR REFLECTION AND LARGE GROUP DISCUSSION

- How would I describe my style of communication?

- What are the similarities in my communication style(s) to the styles of other participants?

- What are the differences in my communication style(s) from the styles of other participants?

■ Which of Taylor's suggestions on effective cross-cultural communication do I find the easiest to follow?

■ Which of these suggestions do I find the hardest to follow?

Cooperative Learning

Approximate time: one to two class sessions

Cooperative learning is the ability to work successfully with other people to solve a problem or complete a task. Communities depend on cooperative learning to survive and to thrive. Cooperation has been called the friendliest of human relationships (Allport, 1954/ 1979) and defined as one of the primary qualities that makes a good citizen (Ohio State Department of Education, 1985).

Classrooms can be competitive spaces, in which students are in direct struggle with each other for grades and individual attention. To build community in the classroom, students and teachers need a different focus. Every student—not just a few star students—needs to have the opportunity to speak and to receive attention for who he or she is.

The classroom contains the reality and the possibility of many different relationships, cooperative as well as competitive. In a program that relies on team teaching and on large and small group discussions and exercises, cooperative relationships can grow alongside competitive ones.

QUESTIONS FOR REFLECTION AND
LARGE GROUP DISCUSSION

■ What is my experience with competition in the classroom?

■ What is my experience with cooperation in the classroom?

■ What can I do to work more cooperatively with other participants?

Small Group Exercise:
Communication, Culture, and Identity

Approximate time: two class sessions

Culture and communication are closely related to individual identity, the characteristics that make a person his or her unique self. In this exercise, participants reflect privately on what has formed their individual identities, then discuss their reflections with other participants in small group sessions.

SUPPLIES: One copy of the form shown in Figure 2.2 for each participant; poster paper and marking pens.

STUDENT LEADERSHIP: At least two students volunteer to help distribute forms and divide participants into small groups. One student in each group then volunteers to take notes on the group's discussion. These notes will be transferred to poster paper for classroom display.

TO BEGIN: The participants take 15 to 20 minutes to complete the form shown in Figure 2.2. On this form, each participant lists in order of importance the communities that helped to form his or her identity at three different stages of life: early childhood, elementary school, and high school.

The exercise leaders then ask the participants to separate into small groups of three to six individuals, using one of the following methods (the participants can take a voice or hand vote on which method they prefer):

By birth order—oldest children, middle children, youngest children, and only children.

By birth months—January, February, March, April, May, June, July, August, September, October, November, December, or any combination of months.

By favorite food, favorite musical artist, or another method suggested by participants.

After assembling in small groups, participants discuss the following questions.

QUESTIONS FOR REFLECTION AND
SMALL GROUP DISCUSSION

- What have been the main influences in forming my individual identity?
- How have the influences on my identity changed during the three stages of my life?
- What are the similarities between what has helped to form my identity and what has helped to form the identities of the other people in my group?
- What are the differences between what has helped to form my identity and what has helped to form the identities of the other people in my group?

Figure 2.2. Communication, Culture, and Identity

From Ages 1 to 5	*From Ages 6 to 12*	*From Ages 13 to 17*
1.	1.	1.
2.	2.	2.
3.	3.	3.
4.	4.	4.
5.	5.	5.

INFLUENCES: Family (specify), neighbors, friends, teachers, ministers/priests, boyfriends/girlfriends, economic status, race, gender, religion, nationality, age, physical ability/disability, other ability/disability, television, movies, music, magazines, books, politics, and other.

At the conclusion of the small group discussions, the recorder in each small group summarizes the group's discussion on poster paper and posts it on the wall. The participants then mingle in the classroom for 10 to 20 minutes, reading the summaries of the other groups.

Critical Thinking and I-Search

Approximate time: two class sessions

Critical thinking is the ability to make an informed judgment. An informed judgment is based on *evidence* rather than on *prejudice*—a word that literally means prejudgment, to judge without evidence. Individual identities can change and grow when individuals develop the ability to think critically about their lived experience, the influences that have shaped their attitudes and behaviors.

Lived experience provides two main sources of evidence for critical thinking. The first is an individual's own lived experience. The second is the lived experience of other people, which can be examined by listening to them speak in person or on radio or on video or audio recordings, by reading their writings, or by watching them on video or film.

Edward D'Angelo (1971) defines 10 habits of mind that develop critical thinking:

1. Intellectual curiosity—asking why, how, who, when, and where

2. Objectivity—relying on the evidence first

3. Open-mindedness—realizing that any piece of evidence may be true, and remembering to review evidence carefully before making a decision

4. Flexibility—being willing to change the way one looks at the evidence before making a judgment

5. Intellectual skepticism—waiting until all of the evidence is in before making a judgment

6. Intellectual honesty—making judgments based on honest consideration of the evidence, not on past opinions

7. Being systematic—following the evidence through to a conclusion without being too distracted by other things

8. Persistence—not giving up until all the evidence is located and considered

9. Decisiveness—being able to make a decision after having located and considered all of the evidence

10. Respect for other viewpoints—realizing that not everyone will make the same decisions; reviewing other people's decisions and in some cases being willing to change one's own

To D'Angelo's (1971) list, we add an 11th habit:

11. Compassion—remembering that understanding other people's motives is part of respect. Being able to recognize and apologize when judgments, even informed judgments, have hurt someone else

I-search is a tool for critical thinking, a form of personal research. In doing I-search, the researcher keeps in mind three main questions: What do I know? What do I need to know? How will I know? These questions can be applied to any research question. The evidence gathered through I-search comes from one's own lived experience and from the lived experience of others, gathered from conversations and interviews; from books, newspapers, and magazines; or from television, video, and music.

QUESTIONS FOR REFLECTION AND LARGE GROUP DISCUSSION

- When have I relied on critical thinking and I-search to address a question or problem?
- When have I ignored critical thinking and I-search in addressing a question or problem?
- Which of the suggestions on critical thinking and I-search do I find the easiest to follow?
- Which of these suggestions do I find the hardest to follow?

Large Group Exercise: Critical Thinking and I-Search in Action

---

Approximate time: two class sessions

This exercise is designed to demonstrate how critical thinking and I-search can broaden participants' understanding of the subject of dealing with differences.

SUPPLIES: Chalkboard and chalk or poster paper and marking pens.

STUDENT LEADERSHIP: One student volunteers to be the recorder for this exercise.

TO BEGIN: The recorder writes three headings on the chalkboard or poster paper: WHAT DO WE KNOW? WHAT DO WE NEED TO KNOW? HOW WILL WE KNOW?

The participants begin by listing the things they already know about dealing with differences. The recorder writes these down under WHAT DO WE KNOW?

The participants then list the things they need to know about dealing with differences. The recorder writes these down under WHAT DO WE NEED TO KNOW?

The participants then list the methods they can use to learn what they need to know about dealing with differences. The recorder writes these down under HOW WILL WE KNOW?

The participants then volunteer to I-search one or more of the questions left unanswered about the program. Students can work on these questions individually or in groups, with or without the help of teachers. In the next class session, the participants report on the results of their I-searches.

Multiple Intelligences

Approximate time: one class session

How an individual defines intelligence plays a major role in his or her critical thinking. In the classroom, intelligence is often measured by the ability to perform well on examinations and on written assignments.

Beginning in the 1980s, some teachers and writers began to look at intelligence differently. They defined seven—and more recently eight—different kinds of intelligence. They saw that every student has strength in at least one area of intelligence and possibly in several areas of intelligence.

The first seven multiple intelligences (Gardner, 1993) are linguistic intelligence, logical-mathematical intelligence, bodily-kinesthetic intelligence, spatial intelligence, musical intelligence, interpersonal intelligence, intrapersonal intelligence. The eighth multiple intelligence (Armstrong, 1994) is naturalistic intelligence.

Linguistic intelligence is skill in using words and language, both in writing and in speaking. Poets and journalists demonstrate strong linguistic intelligence. Linguistic intelligence—primarily in writing—has been traditionally valued in the classroom.

Logical-mathematical intelligence is skill in using numbers and symbols and in logical reasoning. Mathematicians and detectives demonstrate strong logical-mathematical intelligence. Logical-mathematical intelligence—primarily for solving math problems, not for detective reasoning—has been traditionally valued in the classroom.

Bodily-kinesthetic intelligence is skill in using the body through strength and coordination. Athletes, craftspeople, and surgeons demonstrate strong bodily-kinesthetic intelligence. Although bodily-kinesthetic intelligence is valued on the playground and in the gym, and sometimes in the art room, it has not been much valued in the classroom.

Spatial intelligence is the ability to imagine and move objects through space in the mind. Pilots, architects, painters, and people who almost never get lost demonstrate strong spatial intelligence. Except in the art room and in certain specialized courses such as mechanical drafting, spatial intelligence has not been much valued in the classroom.

Musical intelligence is skill in discerning the pitch, rhythm, timbre, and tone of music. Composers, musicians, singers, and people who love music demonstrate strong musical intelligence. Except in the music room, musical intelligence has not been much valued in the classroom.

Interpersonal intelligence is skill in understanding and interacting with other people. Politicians, actors, and even teachers demonstrate strong interpersonal intelligence. Despite the important role it plays in our everyday lives, interpersonal intelligence has not been much valued in the classroom.

Intrapersonal intelligence is skill in understanding oneself and the deep issues of what it means to be human. Religious people, psychologists, and philosophers demonstrate strong intrapersonal intelligence. Sometimes mistaken for shyness or daydreaming, intrapersonal intelligence has not been much valued in the classroom.

Naturalistic intelligence is skill in appreciating the natural world of animals and plants. Biologists, park rangers, gardeners, and people who love the outdoors demonstrate strong naturalistic intelligence. Because the natural world is usually seen as something that stays outside the classroom, naturalistic intelligence has not been much valued in the classroom.

Large Group Exercise: "Who Do I Know Who . . . ?"

Approximate time: one class session

This exercise is designed to help participants discover the different interests and abilities—what are now called multiple intelligences—that exist among the individuals in the classroom.

SUPPLIES: A copy of the form shown in Figure 2.3 for every participant; chalkboard and chalk or poster paper and marking pens.

STUDENT LEADERSHIP: Two students volunteer to help distribute forms, give instructions for this exercise, and record the results of the large group discussion on the chalkboard or poster paper.

TO BEGIN: The exercise leaders give the participants their forms and ask them to circulate through the classroom, talking to one another, until they have answers to at least 13 of the 16 questions on the sheet. Each participant needs to talk to as many individuals as possible in filling out the sheet, because every participant should appear on someone else's sheet at least once. After the sheets are completed, the participants return to their seats for discussion.

QUESTIONS FOR REFLECTION AND LARGE GROUP DISCUSSION

- What are my strongest multiple intelligences?
- In what ways are my multiple intelligences different from those of other participants?
- In what ways are my multiple intelligences similar to those of other participants?
- How might school be different if all of the multiple intelligences were valued in the classroom?
- What surprised me about this exercise?

Guidelines for Interaction in the Classroom

Approximate time: one class session

Guidelines for interaction in the classroom, guidelines that all participants help to develop and agree to follow, are necessary for participants to handle the conflicts that arise in discussing sensitive issues such as race, gender, class, and disability.

The following guidelines (Creighton & Kivel, 1992) are provided as suggestions. Participants can use them, discard them, or add to them as needed.

Amnesty—No one blames or punishes someone for what they said in class.

Put-ups, not put-downs—No one puts anyone down, including himself or herself.

Right to pass—No one is forced to participate.

Respect and listening—One person talks at a time, and other people listen to what that person has to say.

Figure 2.3. Who Do I Know Who . . . ?

1. _____ likes word games like Scrabble or Password.

2. _____ can easily add and subtract in his or her head.

3. _____ likes to draw or doodle.

4. _____ likes roller coasters or other daredevil rides.

5. _____ plays a musical instrument.

6. _____ likes to play group sports like basketball or volleyball.

7. _____ keeps a private journal or diary.

8. _____ likes shows and exhibits about science and nature.

9. _____ likes to make up rhymes, puns, and poems.

10. _____ likes to look for logical explanations for things.

11. _____ has a good sense of direction, even in unfamiliar places.

12. _____ is very well coordinated.

13. _____ knows the tunes to many different songs.

14. _____ likes parties and other social activities.

15. _____ likes to spend time alone thinking or meditating.

16. _____ likes to grow plants, vegetables, or flowers.

I-statements—Each person speaks for himself or herself, from lived experience ("I feel . . .", "I think . . . ").

Try on the process—Each person agrees to give the guidelines a chance, at least as long as the class is in session.

One guideline that we tried to introduce during our pilot program Dealing With Prejudice was confidentiality (no one speaks outside of class about what was said in class). Confidentiality was so frequently broken that it became both meaningless and a source of bitterness to some students. Instead of confidentiality, we suggest the following guideline:

Discretion—Each person exercises care in what he or she says about what went on in class outside the class, remembering to respect the feelings of other individuals.

Large Group Exercise: Developing Guidelines for Interaction

Approximate time: one class session

In this exercise, participants develop guidelines for their group interaction for the remainder of their use of *Dealing With Differences*.

SUPPLIES: Poster board, marking pens.

STUDENT LEADERSHIP: At least two students volunteer to help lead discussion and to record results.

TO BEGIN: The participants suggest guidelines for interaction in their classroom, keeping in mind the suggestions made in the previous section. The recorders write down these suggestions. When all suggestions have been made, the participants review the guidelines for repetitions. They then take a voice or hand vote on each of the guidelines.

When the participants are in agreement on the guidelines, the recorders make a clean copy on poster board and post the guidelines in plain view in the classroom.

Reflection

Approximate time: one class session

Reflection is a conversation with oneself, a private inner dialogue. It begins by simply recalling the details of an experience. It continues as the person who is reflecting considers, What meaning does this experience hold for me? These meanings can be deeply personal. Sometimes they are shared and sometimes they are kept to oneself.

Dealing With Differences contains several readings that participants reflect on in the light of their own lived experience. Participants are invited to put their reflections into a form that displays the multiple intelligences with which they are gifted. A reflection can take the form of an essay, a poem, a rap, a song, a dance, a drawing, an equation, a journal entry, a video, or an image.

Reflections may be used in group exhibits or displays, in presentations or assemblies, or in individual portfolios. Or they may remain private, known to the individual alone.

In preparing their reflections, participants keep in mind the following questions:

QUESTIONS FOR READING AND REFLECTION

- What emotions did this reading evoke in me?
- What lived experience (mine or someone else's) did this reading make me remember?
- What did the reading tell me that I already know and think is important?
- What did the reading tell me that I didn't know and want to know more about?

The poems and essays included in this book may be read aloud in class (or signed, using American Sign Language) if participants feel that doing so would deepen their responses to the readings.

In the next class sessions, participants volunteer to share their reflections. Every participant should have a chance to share his or her reflection, although not every participant may choose to do so.

Individual Exercise:
Reading and Reflection—"Ending Poem"

Approximate time: two class sessions

The next two class sessions will be devoted to sharing reflections on "Ending Poem," by Rosario Morales and Aurora Levins Morales.

Ending Poem*

Rosario Morales and Aurora Levins Morales

Rosario Morales and Aurora Levins Morales are mother and daughter. Rosario Morales, born in Puerto Rico, was raised in New

York City. She returned to Puerto Rico with her Jewish American husband and gave birth to Aurora Levins Morales, who spent her early childhood on a coffee farm. Both poets now live in the mainland United States. In "Ending Poem," they use two voices to explore and celebrate the different cultures that have shaped their identities.

I AM WHAT I AM.
A child of the Americas.
A light-skinned mestiza of the Caribbean.
A child of many diaspora, born into this continent at a
    crossroads.
I am Puerto Rican. I am U.S. American.
I am New York Manhattan and the Bronx.
A mountain-born, country-bred, homegrown jibara child,
up from the shtetl, a California Puerto Rican Jew
A product of the New York ghettos I have never known.
I am an immigrant
and the daughter and granddaughter of immigrants.
We didn't know our forbears' names with a certainty.
They aren't written anywhere.

First names only or mija, negra, ne, honey, sugar, dear
I come from the dirt where the cane was grown.
My people didn't go to dinner parties. They weren't invited.
I am caribeña, island grown.
Spanish is in my flesh, ripples from my tongue, lodges in
    my hips,
the language of garlic and mangoes.
Boricua. As boricuas come from the isle of Manhattan.
I am of latinoamerica, rooted in the history of my
    continent.
I speak from that body. Just brown and pink and full of
    drums inside.

I am not African.
Africa waters the roots of my tree, but I cannot return.

I am not Taina.
I am a late leaf of that ancient tree,
and my roots reach into the soil of two Americas.
Taino is in me, but there is no way back.

---

*"Ending Poem," from *Getting Home Alive* by Rosario Morales and Aurora Levins Morales. Ithaca, New York: Firebrand Books. © 1986 by Aurora Levins Morales and Rosario Morales. Reprinted with permission.

I am not European, though I have dreamt of those cities.
Each plate is different.
wood, clay, papier maché, metals basketry, a leaf, a
    coconut shell.
Europe lives in me but I have no home there.

The table has a cloth woven by one, dyed by another,
embroidered by another still.
I am a child of many mothers.
They have kept it all going

All the civilizations erected on their backs.
All the dinner parties given with their labor.

We are new.
They gave us life, kept us going,
brought us to where we are.
Born at a crossroads.
Come, lay that dishcloth down. Eat, dear, eat.

History made us.
We will not eat ourselves up inside anymore.

And we are whole.

3

Class and Classism

It's realizing what goes on. A lot of people here are sheltered, but then some of them are exposed to the elements. Every hour of every day —I know there's people here, they only have one skirt, one shirt. Go home and wash it in the sink. There's people here on every plank of society and they're all together, and you just have to make it.

—student from pilot program Dealing With Prejudice

Class *has been defined since the late 18th to mid-19th century as the division of society into social and economic ranks or orders (New Shorter Oxford English Dictionary, 1993). These "planks of society," as our student put it, form a complex structure of relationships among individuals as well as among groups. Class is not only an issue of money, but an issue of power and influence, including factors such as education, occupation, race, gender, and disability.*

In the United States today, new definitions of class are being developed to account for the economic hardship, decline, and uncertainty faced by millions of Americans (Dolbeare & Hubbell, 1996) as the United States shifts from an industrial economy to a postindustrial economy based on the production of services and knowledge

(Howe, 1992). New definitions of class also take into account the role of class—along with race and gender—in the inequalities that exist in schooling (Stevenson & Ellsworth, 1993; Weis, 1993).

Using the exercises, discussion topics, and reading in this chapter, participants explore their own ideas and feelings about class and difference, the construction of class, classism and its relationships to other prejudices, individual experiences with class, and suggestions for action on class issues in the classroom and community.

This chapter contains the following sections. The times given to complete them are approximate.

Icebreaker: "How the Cookie Crumbles" (two class sessions)
What Is Class? (two class sessions)
Large Group Exercise: CLASS DIFFERENCE and VALUE (one class session)
Classism (two to three class sessions)
Individual Exercise: Media Images of Class (one to two class sessions)
Large Group Exercise: Common Ground on Class (one to two class sessions)
Small Group Exercise: Class—Concerns and Suggestions for Action (two class sessions)
Large Group Exercise: Class—Concerns and Suggestions for Action (two class sessions)
Guest Speaker on Class (one to two class sessions)
Individual Exercise: Reading and Reflection—"There's Me" (two class sessions)

Icebreaker: "How the Cookie Crumbles"

Approximate time: two class sessions

What do facts and figures about class differences in the United States really mean to the people behind the statistics? How does it feel to be rich? How does it feel to be poor?

"How the Cookie Crumbles" is an exercise designed to help participants experience in a personal way the significant differences in ownership of private wealth in today's United States (see Figure 3.1). As with other exercises in *Dealing With Differences,* "How the Cookie Crumbles" depends on the participants being respectful of each other and assuming responsibility for the process.

SUPPLIES: Box of large, soft cookies equal to number of participants; sheets of yellow, orange, and gray construction paper; scissors; photocopy enlargement of Figure 3.1 to display in class; paper

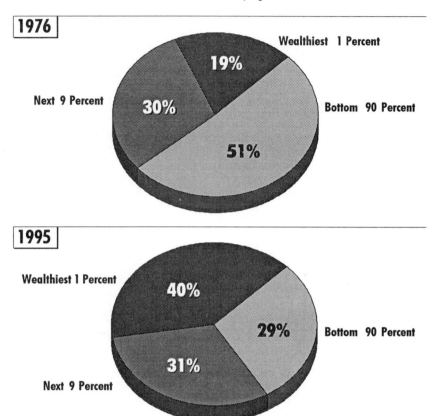

The Top 1% of wealth holders took a bigger share of the pie.
The Bottom 90% were very big losers.

1976

Wealthiest 1 Percent

19%

Next 9 Percent

30%

Bottom 90 Percent

51%

1995

Wealthiest 1 Percent

40%

Bottom 90 Percent

29%

Next 9 Percent

31%

Figure 3.1. Ownership of Private Wealth in the United States
SOURCE: United for a Fair Economy, Boston, MA (1995). Reprinted with permission.

bag (a decorated paper bag would enhance the fun of this exercise); chalkboard and chalk or poster paper and marking pens.

STUDENT LEADERSHIP: At least two students volunteer to help prepare the tokens for this game, pass out paper tokens and cookies, and record the results of the large group discussion on the chalkboard or poster paper.

PREPARATION (done before class): The exercise leaders cut the sheets of yellow, orange, and gray construction paper into small pieces or tokens. There should be one token for each student and teacher in the class. Tokens of yellow ("gold") construction paper represent the top 1% of wealth holders in the United

States; tokens of gray ("silver") construction paper represent the second 9% of wealth holders, and tokens of orange ("copper") construction paper represent the bottom 90% of wealth holders.

The exercise leaders need to bend percentages a little in preparing tokens for this exercise. There should be at least two participants in each group. To give an example: In a class of 30 participants, 2 individuals—not the 0.3% of a person that literally represents 1% of the class—get gold tokens, 4 individuals get silver tokens, and 22 individuals get copper tokens.

After preparing and counting the tokens, the exercise leaders place the tokens in the paper bag.

The exercise leaders divide the cookies strictly according to the percentage of private wealth that each of the three groups will own, breaking them into pieces to ensure accurate distribution. To give an example: In a class of 30 participants, 12 cookies (30 × .40) go to the gold group; 9.3 cookies (30 × .31) go to the silver group, and 8.7 cookies (30 × .29) go to the copper group.

To Begin: The exercise leaders call the participants' attention to Figure 3.1 and explain that in this exercise the members of the class represent the population of the United States as divided by wealth into the top 1%, the next 9%, and the bottom 90%. They ask the participants to each take one token from the paper bag. They then ask the participants to divide into groups (those with gold tokens at the front of the room, those with silver tokens at the middle of the room, and those with copper tokens at the back of the room).

The exercise leaders then distribute to each group the cookies that it "owns."

The three groups engage in discussion of the following questions.

QUESTIONS FOR DISCUSSION IN THE THREE GROUPS

- How do we feel about being in our group?
- What do we feel about the other groups?
- What can we do about our situation?

After all participants have had a chance to strategize, they return to their seats for discussion in the group as a whole.

QUESTIONS FOR REFLECTION AND LARGE GROUP DISCUSSION

- How did it feel to be in my group?
- What did my group do with the wealth it had?
- What could my group have done with the wealth it had?
- What surprised me about this exercise?

Strategies that have been used by previous participants in this exercise include:

Dividing the cookies equally among group members

Dividing the cookies unequally among group members

Hoarding cookies

Asking or negotiating for cookies from another group

Giving cookies to another group, either voluntarily or as a result of negotiation

After reviewing these strategies, the participants may want to do the exercise again. If this option is chosen, the participants can reassemble in their previous small groups or start the exercise from the beginning.

What Is Class?

Approximate time: two class sessions

Class is difficult to define because the United States has an image as a classless society (Stevenson & Ellsworth, 1993), one in which every individual has an opportunity to succeed. The class with which many Americans identify—regardless of their financial or social status—is the middle class. The values that attracted immigrants to the United States and built the American Dream are middle-class values: individualism, opportunity, property, freedom, and equality (Dolbeare & Hubbell, 1996).

When the writer bell hooks (1994) told a friend that her family was poor, he corrected her, saying that her family was working class. The refusal of hooks's friend to identify someone he liked as poor is evidence that class is not just a matter of money but of values. In one sense, class is a *construct,* a social concept or idea. Constructs about class—as about race, gender, and disability—help individuals and groups to make sense of their world, as well as to gain social and economic control of their world. In viewing class as a construct, the focus is on how real differences in wealth or status are influenced by the ways in which value is assigned to those differences—the value assigned to a doctor as opposed to the value assigned to a janitor, for example (Rothenberg, 1992). Acknowledging difference is merely saying that X is different from Y; assigning value to difference is saying that X is superior or inferior to Y.

The stories of people who have risen from rags to riches have long been popular in U.S. culture. These are sometimes called Horatio Alger stories or the Horatio Alger myth, after a 19th-century author of best-selling novels, Horatio Alger. Alger's heroes were virtuous and ambitious young men who started their work lives by selling newspapers or shining shoes on street corners and ended up owning large businesses (Nackenoff, 1994).

If to succeed economically is to embody the American Dream, then to fail is to embody its opposite. The anti-Horatio Alger exists in stereotypes of the unsuccessful person as stupid, immoral, welfare dependent, and shiftless (Dolbeare & Hubbell, 1996).

Class constructs serve to justify a concrete system in which money and power are distributed unequally. The United States has been and remains a country with serious class differences. The lower and middle classes have lost ground since the 1970s as wealth has become concentrated in the hands of the top 1% to 5% of the U.S. population. The United States also has the greatest income inequality of any industrialized nation (Dolbeare & Hubbell, 1996).

The decline of the U.S. steel industry in the 1970s signaled a shift in the U.S. economy from industrial to postindustrial, resulting in large-scale changes in the number and type of jobs available to workers. Between 1982 and 1995, the number of new and replacement jobs for traditional low-status positions—custodians, cashiers, and sales clerks—was estimated at 10 to 15 million. The number of new and replacement jobs for computer programmers, systems analysts, and electrical engineers was estimated at only 500,000 to 700,000 (Weis, 1993). The much-talked-about class of skilled technical workers—what Carolyn Howe (1992) calls knowledge controllers—is and will remain much smaller than the traditional classes of manual and clerical workers.

Howe (1992) defines eight class categories in the United States today. At the top she places capitalists—those who, like Horatio Alger's heroes, control money, property, businesses, and power. The other chasses include petit bourgeois (the lower middle classes); knowledge controllers; semiprofessionals; managers; supervisors; clerical workers; and at the bottom, manual workers.

hooks (1994), drawing on her lived experience as an African-American child in the Kentucky of the 1950s and 1960s, breaks down class into four basic categories: the poor, struggling working folks, working folks with extra money, and the rich. The line between poor and struggling working folks, in hooks's view, is thin:

"Technically we *were* working class, because my father worked as a janitor at the post office, however the fact that there were seven children in our family meant that we often faced economic hardship in ways that made us children at least think of ourselves as poor" (p. 166).

Who are the poor? The number of Americans defined by the government as living in poverty was 39,265,000 in 1993—nearly one in seven Americans. Poor Americans included 15,727,000 people under the age of 18 (U.S. Bureau of the Census, 1995).

Who are the struggling working folks? Some of them are found among the poor. Katherine Newman (1996) estimates that 30 million Americans hold minimum-wage, low-status jobs in places such as restaurants, hospitals, and hotels. In studying low-wage workers in the largely African-American New York City neighborhood of Harlem, Newman found that although 67% of households included at least one full-time worker, 40% of the population still existed below the poverty line. She also found that for every 14 individuals seeking jobs there was only one job available.

Even those workers who make more than $5 or $6 dollars an hour may be struggling. A "good job" is defined by Dolbeare and Hubbell (1996, p. 89) as one that pays a minimum of $12 to $15 an hour ($25,000 to $30,000 a year in 1992 dollars); includes health care, vacations, other standard benefits; and provides safe and satisfying working conditions.

Who are the working folks with extra money? A good job of $25,000 to $30,000 a year may just cover necessities and emergencies for a family. In the 1980s, the annual wage increase for workers who made $20,000 to $50,000 a year was 4%, not enough to cover increases in the cost of living. The annual wage increase for workers who made between $200,000 and $1 million a year, however, was 69% (Barlett & Steele, 1992).

Who are the rich? The annual wage increase in the 1980s for those who made over $1 million dollars a year was 210%. The amount of money earned by the top 4% of U.S. workers by 1989 was as much as the bottom 51% of U.S. workers combined (Barlett & Steele, 1992).

QUESTIONS FOR REFLECTION AND LARGE GROUP DISCUSSION

- How do I describe myself by class?
- Who and what has influenced my thoughts and feelings about class?
- Have changes in jobs and class structure during the past 20 years affected me, my family, and my friends? How?
- What constructs of class have I used to make sense of my world or to control my world?

Large Group Exercise: CLASS DIFFERENCE and VALUE

Approximate time: one class session

In this exercise, participants examine the class differences that exist in society and the values assigned to those differences through constructs of class.

SUPPLIES: Chalkboard and chalk or poster paper and marking pens.

STUDENT LEADERSHIP: One student volunteers to be the recorder for this exercise.

TO BEGIN: The recorder writes the words CLASS DIFFERENCE and VALUE at the head of two different columns on the chalkboard or poster paper.

Participants suggest words or phrases that express the class differences that they have observed in society. The recorder writes these words and phrases in the CLASS DIFFERENCE column.

Participants suggest words or phrases that express the values that they have observed being assigned to these differences. The recorder writes these words and phrases in the VALUE column.

QUESTIONS FOR REFLECTION AND LARGE GROUP DISCUSSION

- What class differences do I see in my community or society?
- What values do I assign to those differences?
- What surprised me about this exercise?

Classism

Approximate time: two to three class sessions

Classism, a term dating from the mid-19th century, refers to both the belief that some classes are inferior to others and the practices of discrimination and violence based on that belief (*New Shorter Oxford English Dictionary,* 1993). Classism is rooted in both the constructs of class and the fundamental inequities of money and power in U.S. society.

The three categories of racism defined by Joseph Barndt (1991) and discussed in Chapter 4 can also be applied to classism: *individual classism,* the prejudices held by a particular person; *cultural classism,* the prejudices held by members of a particular culture or community; and *institutional classism,* a system of economic and social discrimination against persons belonging to the lower classes. Institutional classism, like institutional racism, is "prejudice plus power" (Barndt, 1991, p. 28).

In individual classism, persons believe and act on constructs of class learned from their communities. Both individuals who identify themselves as upper or middle class and individuals who identify themselves as working class or lower class can internalize—take within themselves—classist constructs. In a study of working-class high school dropouts, Stevenson and Ellsworth (1993) found that the students blamed themselves wholly for their failures, internalizing classist constructs of themselves as lazy, stupid, and worthless. In their self-blame, the students abandoned the sharp critiques they had made earlier of their school and teachers as being inadequate to their needs, particularly in a postindustrial society with fewer and fewer well-paying jobs.

Economic insecurity can turn individual classism outward. Lois Weis (1993) found in a study of white working-class males that they vented their fears and frustrations about their own uncertain futures in prejudice toward white women and men and women of color.

An example of individual classism raised during our pilot program Dealing With Prejudice is judging persons on what William James called the material self—body, clothes, and possessions (Kaiser, 1990). In her post-program interview, a student spoke of being snubbed by classmates because she could not afford the kind of clothes and shoes that were popular. A teacher spoke in class of being hurt when during a visit to an old friend to talk about his father's death he noticed the friend looking out the window, trying to gauge the teacher's success by seeing what make of car he was driving.

Cultural classism is built on the construct of the superiority of upper- or middle-class individuals and values and the inferiority of working-class or lower-class individuals and values. The Horatio Alger myth, in which success rests solely on the ambition and hard work of the individual, is a prime example of cultural classism. This myth is used to justify and dismiss the existence of the poor and struggling: If only they were willing to work harder, they could make it. Stevenson and Ellsworth (1993) attribute to the "culture of individualism" (p. 271) the destruction of working-class solidarity and pride among the high school dropouts they studied, a loss made more poignant by the fact that the students had learned nothing about labor history or unions in school.

Institutional classism refers to class inequities that are deeply entrenched in the social and economic systems of the United States. The striking inequalities in income and wealth discussed earlier in this chapter and shown in Figure 3.1 are examples of institutional classism. The fact that businesses such as grocery stores and banks often refuse to stay in poorer urban neighborhoods, that these neighborhoods often receive less police protection than other neighborhoods, and that the people who live in them often pay higher insurance rates—examples given by Barndt (1991) of institutional racism—are also examples of institutional classism.

Another example of institutional classism is ability grouping and tracking in education (Oakes, 1985). Although some individuals defend tracking as necessary to groom potential leaders in science, government, and business, tracking stereotypes the majority of students as less able. Poor and minority students are placed in low-ability groups more often than middle-class and nonminority students.

Our pilot program Dealing With Prejudice was implemented in the one untracked class in an otherwise tracked curriculum. Some of the tensions we dealt with in the course of the program had to do with ability grouping, as students in the lower ability groups began to express themselves more often and more confidently, unsettling students in the high ability group, who were not used to competing with these students to be heard. Tracking issues surfaced in several post-program interviews. We were told that only one of our African-American students—out of nearly 20—was in the high ability group. Several students, both European-American and African-American, expressed frustration over ability grouping and the quality of education that they were receiving. They mentioned ability grouping as a factor in their decisions to transfer to other schools.

QUESTIONS FOR REFLECTION AND LARGE GROUP DISCUSSION

■ What lived experience do I have with individual classism?

■ What lived experience do I have with cultural classism?

■ What lived experience do I have with institutional classism?

■ What relationships do I see between classism and other prejudices?

Individual Exercise: Media Images of Class

Approximate time: one to two class sessions

What cultural images of class exist in the mass media—newspapers, magazines, books, movies, television, music? What constructs of class do these images portray?

In this exercise, participants can choose to do one, two, or all three of the following out-of-class assignments to explore the ways in which class is portrayed in our society.

OPTION A: Select one image (photograph, advertisement, illustration, political cartoon) that expresses something you find significant about class or the constructs of class discussed in this chapter. Prepare a brief oral or written reflection on the image to share in class.

OPTION B: Watch television over the course of a week and note how persons of different social and economic classes are portrayed in commercials, drama shows, comedy shows, and documentaries or news broadcasts. Prepare a brief oral or written report to share in class.

OPTION C: Review a fairy tale or other children's story and note how it portrays persons of different social and economic classes. Prepare a brief oral or written report to share in class.

In the next class or classes, each participant needs to have the opportunity to share his or her report, although not everyone may choose to speak. After the sharing of reports is completed, the participants may choose to make a collage or display of their images and reports in the classroom or in another area of the school.

QUESTIONS FOR REFLECTION AND LARGE GROUP DISCUSSION

- What constructs of class are displayed by the medium I chose to report on (image, television programs, fairy tale or children's story)?

- How are the constructs I discovered similar to the constructs discovered by other participants?

- How are the constructs I discovered different from those discovered by other participants?

- What surprised me about this exercise?

Large Group Exercise: Common Ground on Class

Approximate time: one to two class sessions

What concerns do participants have and want to share about issues of class? Common Ground, an exercise adapted from Share the Wealth/United for a Fair Economy in Boston, Massachusetts, is designed to encourage the sharing of thoughts and feelings about a particular issue. As with other exercises in *Dealing With Differences,* Common Ground depends on the participants being respectful of each other and assuming responsibility for the process.

SUPPLIES: Chalkboard and chalk or poster paper and marking pens.

STUDENT LEADERSHIP: Two or more students volunteer to begin the sharing of concerns and to record a summary of the concerns and of the large group discussion on the chalkboard or poster paper.

TO BEGIN: The participants form a circle. One person then volunteers to be the first to share a concern he or she has about the topic under discussion. This person moves inside the circle and speaks the concern.

Here are some examples of concerns about class taken from our pilot program Dealing With Prejudice:

I'm concerned because my sister only makes minimum wage and she has a baby to support.

I'm concerned because I've put in 20 applications and I still can't find a job.

I'm concerned because people in school make fun of me because I can't afford the kind of clothes and shoes that are popular.

Participants who feel that they share the concern expressed—who identify with the speaker because similar things have happened to them or to people they care about—join the speaker inside the circle. These participants can exchange greetings and speak about their identification with the concern if they wish.

After a few minutes, all of these participants move back to the large circle and another person moves inside the circle to state a concern. This person is joined by the individuals who share his or her concern. After a few minutes of conversation, these participants move back.

The process of sharing concerns continues until everyone has had the opportunity to speak, although not everyone may decide to speak.

The participants return to their seats. They take five to ten minutes to summarize the concerns raised in the exercise. An exercise leader records this summary on the chalkboard or poster paper.

QUESTIONS FOR REFLECTION AND
LARGE GROUP DISCUSSION

- Which concerns do I identify or agree with?
- Which concerns do I not identify or agree with?

- How did I feel about the way other participants responded to my concerns?

- What surprised me about this exercise?

Small Group Exercise: Class— Concerns and Suggestions for Action

Approximate time: two class sessions

What concerns about class are most important to the participants? What actions can they take to address these concerns? To explore these questions, in this exercise the participants assemble in the small groups formed in Chapter 2.

Action can take a variety of forms, both individual and collective. It is important that the actions students suggest—however small or incremental—are taken seriously by teachers and administrators and encouraged whenever possible. If teachers dismiss or discourage suggestions for action, students may justly complain that the program is hypocritical or irrelevant to their lives. Here are some examples of actions suggested and taken by students in our pilot program Dealing With Prejudice:

1. Speak up more for yourself and for others in the face of prejudice

2. Form an after-school discussion/action group

3. Go as a class or group to a relevant movie and discuss it afterward

4. Watch as a class or group relevant videos or TV programs

5. Read books and magazines about your concern

6. Write or call the local newspaper, radio station, or TV station about your concern

7. Boycott businesses that ignore or contribute to your concern

8. Meet as a group with school administrators about your concern

9. Volunteer with an existing school, church, or community group that works on your concern

10. Hold a student-run school assembly on your concern

11. Develop a play or presentation on your concern and perform it for the entire school

12. Develop a display or exhibit on your concern in the classroom or elsewhere on school property

SUPPLIES: Poster paper and marking pens.

STUDENT LEADERSHIP: One student in each small group volunteers to record the results of the small group's discussion on poster paper.

TO BEGIN: Each small group chooses one concern to explore from the list developed and recorded during Common Ground. The group recorder then puts these four columns on paper:

What do we know (about this concern)?

What do we need to know (about this concern)?

How can we know (about this concern)?

How can we act (on this concern)?

Using as a guideline the principles of critical thinking and I-search described in Chapter 2, each group brainstorms the concern it has chosen. The small groups may consult with teachers on completing this process through trips to the school or the public library or calls or meetings with community members. Teachers and students decide together how much I-search can be done during the *Dealing With Differences* sessions and how much can be done outside of class.

When I-search is completed, the recorder in each small group summarizes the group's findings on a sheet of poster paper and posts it on the wall to be read and considered by other participants.

Large Group Exercise: Class— Concerns and Suggestions for Action

Approximate time: two class sessions

In this exercise, the participants reflect on the results of the small group discussions and decide which suggestions for action they can implement as individuals, as small groups, or as a class.

SUPPLIES: Chalkboard and chalk or poster paper and marking pens.

STUDENT LEADERSHIP: Two or more students volunteer to give instructions for the exercise and to record the results of the large group discussion on the chalkboard or poster paper.

TO BEGIN: The exercise leaders ask the participants to leave their desks to read the posted results of the small group discussions. The participants are encouraged to ask questions of one another and to make notes on what they find interesting.

After 10 to 20 minutes of mingling, the participants return to their seats for discussion.

QUESTIONS FOR REFLECTION AND LARGE GROUP DISCUSSION

- Now that I have reviewed all of the suggestions for action, what suggestions would I most like to implement?

- Are these actions I can take as an individual? As part of a group? As a member of this class?

- What help do I need from other participants (students or teachers) to take action?

- What help do I need from people outside the classroom (administrators, community members, family) to take action?

Guest Speaker on Class

Approximate time: one to two class sessions

At this point, after the participants have discussed class, classism, concerns, and suggestions for action, we recommend that they invite a guest into the classroom to engage in a dialogue with the participants on issues of class. We recommend that the speaker be someone who not only works on issues of class but also has lived experience with these issues. It would be significant if the speaker was a friend or family member of one of the participants.

Local social service organizations and advocacy organizations may be able to provide or to recommend speakers.

Individual Exercise: Reading and Reflection—"There's Me"

Approximate time: two class sessions

For the next class sessions, the participants read "There's Me" by Jimmy Santiago Baca. This poem may be read aloud in class (or signed, using American Sign Language) if participants feel that doing so would deepen their responses to it.

The participants prepare reflections on the reading in a form that displays one or more of their multiple intelligences (see Chapter 2)—an essay, a poem, a rap, a song, a dance, a drawing, an equation, a journal entry, a video, or an image. These reflections may be used in group exhibits or displays, in presentations or assemblies, or in individual portfolios.

In preparing their reflections, participants keep in mind the following questions:

QUESTIONS FOR READING AND REFLECTION

- What emotions did this reading evoke in me?

- What lived experience (mine or someone else's) did this reading make me remember?

- What did the reading tell me that I already know and think is important?

- What did the reading tell me that I didn't know and want to know more about?

In the next class sessions, the participants volunteer to share their reflections. Every participant should have a chance to share his or her reflection, although not every participant may choose to do so.

There's Me*

Jimmy Santiago Baca

Jimmy Santiago Baca is a self-educated poet who taught himself to read while in prison and went on to earn a general equivalency diploma (GED) and win an American Book Award. He lives with his family in Albuquerque, New Mexico. In "There's Me," Santiago Baca explores class differences and inequalities with an emphasis on his characters' resilient spirits.

There's me & Thelma & Louie & Lisa.
We're the kinda people, don't know too much about that
    place.
We know about factories all right, but not about how
    everybody up there makes so much money.
Like Louie says, how you gonna make so much money
if you don't work? And Thelma says, sure people use their
    brains,
but a body works too. But a body costs a nickel, a mind
    costs
a million. And all them minds, what if there weren't no
    bodies to work for them? Huh?
Up in that place, that's really something
uh, Lisa, really something.
Here we are in clothes and talk and faces.
We know what's going on down here, but up there?
    Man . . .

---

*"There's Me" from *What's Happening* by Jimmy Santiago Baca (Curbstone Press, 1982). Used by permission of Curbstone Press. Distributed by Consortium.

So don't ask me why I carry a knife. Like
this, and don't ask me no questions, because I don't
     understand;
but take a cop wants to arrest somebody, and I'm walking
down the street, why me? He just wants to arrest
     somebody.
Not him, but someone told him to arrest somebody. And
     that
someone was told by someone else, who had little
     numbers in
a paper that say things ain't going too well. Now where'd
he get them numbers? Maybe from somebody with a
     computer
up in one of them offices up there. Just a regular old man
or lady standing in front of a machine writing out numbers
and figuring stuff up.
     Now why's he figuring something up? Ok Lisa
look: he's figuring up something, because someone else
wants him to. And you know someone who can make
him figure something up, is somebody big. Way up there ...
probably got a whole bunch of things in this world like
boat companies and oil companies and things like that.
     Just think, why does he want anyone to figure
up something? Cause one of the dudes that work for him
     told
him something was going wrong somewhere, and the
     figuring
needed to be done cuz it was messing things up.
     And how does he know? I think he looks at
all these charts, you know, and if the line goes down, that
means the chump is losing. He's paid to win. So he's got
all these college dudes with degrees, thousands of them,
in a big ole building, working all day, so he can win.
They figure up everything.
     And from way up there, whatever comes out,
on a little piece of paper figured up by a thousand minds,
happens down here on the street. See what I mean?
     We're different man. You go to work Thelma
and spill coffee on tables, collect tips, smoke cigarettes,
you know, you know what's going on with yourself. And I
and Lisa and me, we all live, like getting good clothes,
dressing up for Friday night, riding down Central, getting
up in the morning and cursing at cockroaches, it's a good
life, better, because we know we're human beings. Know
what I mean?
     So there ain't nothing wrong with us man,
we're ok, we're good people, and our life ain't so bad man.
We'll make it, we'll look out for each other.

4

Race, Racism, and Xenophobia

It's your parents who say, "Well, they're wrong," or "They shouldn't be racist" . . . or "I hate black people," or "I hate white people," or "I hate Irish people, or Chinese people." . . . When they say that, that's what their child does. . . . When the child goes out on their own, and learns about the people, they have less hate, but until then, until they get to know the people . . . they probably won't take the time, because their parents told them, "Well, they're bad. Don't be around them."

—student from pilot program Dealing With Prejudice

Race *has been defined since the late 18th century as the division of human beings into distinct ethnic groups that possess particular qualities or characteristics (New Shorter Oxford English Dictionary, 1993). In the United States today, new definitions of race are being developed by the millions of Americans who claim a multiracial identity (Gay, 1995; Mathews, 1996). New definitions of race also take into account the persistence of racial prejudice and violence (Bell, 1992; Kleg, 1993) and the sense of race as a source of personal identity, community, and pride, particularly for people of color (Gay 1995; hooks, 1994).*

Using the exercises, discussion topics, and readings in this chapter, participants will explore their own ideas and feelings about race and difference, the construction of race, racism and its relationship to other prejudices, individual experiences with race, and suggestions for action on racial issues in the classroom and community.

This chapter contains the following sections. The times given to complete them are approximate.

Icebreaker: "Where Are My Roots?" (one to two class sessions)

What Is Race? (two class sessions)

Large Group Exercise: RACIAL DIFFERENCE and VALUE (one class session)

Racism (two to three class sessions)

Individual Exercise: Media Images of Race (one to two class sessions)

Individual Exercise: Reading and Reflection —"Coping With Racism" (two class sessions)

Large Group Exercise: Common Ground on Race (one to two class sessions)

Small Group Exercise: Race—Concerns and Suggestions for Action (two class sessions)

Large Group Exercise: Race—Concerns and Suggestions for Action (two class sessions)

Guest Speaker on Race (one to two class sessions)

Racism and Xenophobia (two class sessions)

Individual Exercise: Reading and Reflection—"Racism Doesn't Grow Up" (two class sessions)

Icebreaker: "Where Are My Roots?"

Approximate time: one to two class sessions

How do individuals define themselves by the regions and countries they or their ancestors came from? How does identification with these heritages influence individual identity?

In the "Where Are My Roots?" exercise, participants examine the similarities and differences in their heritages. As with other exercises in *Dealing With Differences,* "Where Are My Roots?" depends on the participants being respectful of each other and assuming responsibility for the process.

SUPPLIES: Map of the world; box of straight pins; chalkboard and chalk or poster paper and marking pens.

STUDENT LEADERSHIP: Two students volunteer to give instructions for the exercise, to place pins on the map, and to record the results of the large group discussion on the chalkboard or poster paper.

PREPARATION: The exercise leaders put the map of the world on the bulletin board. During the exercise, they place straight pins in the map to mark the places in the world where the participants have roots.

TO BEGIN: The exercise leaders ask the participants to move their desks to create an open space in the middle of the classroom and to form a circle. The exercise leaders then ask the participants to come inside the circle in response to the questions listed below. Participants enter the circle every time they can identify with the roots in question. As the icebreaker progresses, participants may want to add their own questions to the questions asked by the exercise leaders.

After this process is completed, all participants return to their seats for large group discussion.

EXERCISE QUESTIONS

1. Everyone who has Native American/American Indian roots, come into the circle. Say hello.

   Identify yourself by tribes and/or states ("Mohawk from New York State," for example), so that the exercise leaders can place pins in the appropriate places on the map of the world.

   Step out of the circle.

2. Everyone who has European roots, come into the circle. Say hello.

   Identify yourself by countries and/or regions ("Ireland," "Eastern Europe") so that the exercise leaders can place pins in the appropriate places on the map of the world.

   Step out of the circle.

3. Everyone who has African roots, come into the circle. Say hello.

   Identify yourself by countries and/or regions so that the exercise leaders can place pins in the appropriate places on the map of the world.

   Step out of the circle.

4. Everyone who has Central or South American roots, come into the circle. Say hello.

Identify yourself by countries and/or regions so that the exercise leaders can place pins in the appropriate places on the map of the world.

Step out of the circle.

5. Everyone who has Asian roots, come into the circle. Say hello.

    Identify yourself by countries and/or regions so that the exercise leaders can place pins in the appropriate places on the map of the world.

    Step out of the circle.

6. Everyone who has Caribbean roots, come into the circle. Say hello.

    Identify yourself by countries and/or regions so that the exercise leaders can place pins in the appropriate places on the map of the world.

    Step out of the circle.

7. Everyone who has Middle Eastern roots, come into the circle. Say hello.

    Identify yourself by countries and/or regions so that the exercise leaders can place pins in the appropriate places on the map of the world.

    Step out of the circle.

8. Anyone whose roots have not been identified, come into the circle. Say hello.

    Identify yourself by countries and/or regions so that the exercise leaders can place pins in the appropriate places on the map of the world.

    Step out of the circle.

QUESTIONS FOR REFLECTION AND LARGE GROUP DISCUSSION

- How have my roots shaped my sense of who I am?
- What are the similarities between my roots and the roots of other people in the classroom?
- What are the differences between my roots and the roots of other people in the classroom?
- What surprised me about this exercise?

What Is Race?

Approximate time: two class sessions

In addition to its definition as dividing human beings into distinct categories, *race* can be defined as referring to all people, the human race (*New Shorter Oxford English Dictionary*, 1993). All human beings belong to a single species, *Homo sapiens.* Despite obvious physical differences among people from various countries, regions, and continents, pure races do not exist in the human species. The racial categories developed in the late 18th century are merely labels for discussing and comparing the differences among members of the human race (Kleg, 1993).

Race is a *construct,* a social concept or idea. Constructs about race—as about class, gender, and disability—help individuals and groups to make sense of their world, as well as to gain social and economic control of their world.

The key to the construction of race is not the physical or cultural differences that exist among different people, but the ways in which value is assigned to these differences (Rothenberg, 1992). Acknowledging difference is merely saying that X is different from Y; assigning value to difference is saying that X is superior or inferior to Y.

The constructs of race developed by the late 18th century were based on the idea that "white" people were superior and "nonwhite" people —particularly "black" people—were inferior. Scientists and philosophers such as Immanuel Kant, Herbert Spencer, and Charles Darwin explained and justified traditional constructs of race in their work (Kleg, 1993). In 1738, the Swedish botanist Carl von Linné, known as Carolus Linneaus, developed the following classifications of European, American Indian, Asian, and African peoples:

1. Europeaeus albus: White, ruddy, muscular. Abundant yellow hair; blue-eyed. Light, lively (active), ingenious (inventive). Covered with tailored clothes, governed by customs (ruled by rites).

2. Americanius rubesceus: Reddish, choleric [angry], erect. Straight, dense black hair; wide nostrils, freckled face; chin almost beardless. Paints himself with skillful red lines. Ruled by custom.

3. Asiaticus luridus: Yellow, melancholic [sad], inflexible. Black hair; dark eyes. Stern, haughty, stingy (miserly). Covered with loose garments. Ruled by opinion.

4. Afer niger: Black, phlegmatic [passive, slow], indulgent. Black hair, kinky; skin smooth, flat nose, tumid [full] lips. The woman

with a natural apron, the breasts lactating abundantly. Crazy, lazy, negligent. Anoints himself with oil. Governed by whim. (Kleg, 1993, pp. 66-67)

Newer constructs of race challenge the superiority of whiteness. As a result of the black liberation movement of the 1960s and 1970s, bell hooks (1994) states, "The slogan 'black is beautiful' worked to intervene and alter those racist stereotypes that had always insisted black was ugly, monstrous, undesirable" (p. 174). Other liberation movements of the same time period—American Indian, Hispanic, Asian—also challenged the superiority of whiteness and gave individuals a sense of pride in their heritages.

hooks (1994) sees the superiority of whiteness as being reinforced today, in the culture of the 1990s: "The images of black female . . . evil temper, and treachery continue to be marked by darker skin . . . no light skin occupies this devalued position. We see these images continually in the mass media" (p. 179).

A group called Project RACE is lobbying the federal government to add a new category, multiracial, to the national census for the year 2000. (The census has since 1977 used the racial categories white, black, American Indian and Alaska native, and Asian and Pacific islander, with the categories Hispanic or Spanish and other listed separately on the 1990 census.) An estimated 5 million Americans in families where the parents are of different races may be affected by the addition of a multiracial category.

Some Americans of mixed heritages see calling themselves multiracial as a way of breaking down racial barriers and the only true way of describing who they are. Others, however, oppose any classification of people by race other than the human race. Still others, including some American Indian and black activists, see a multiracial classification as a way of reemphasizing the superiority of white heritage over black, American Indian, or Asian heritage and diminishing the power and resources available to minority groups (Mathews, 1996).

QUESTIONS FOR REFLECTION AND LARGE GROUP DISCUSSION

- How do I describe or define myself by race?

- Who and what has influenced my thoughts and feelings about race?

- What constructs of race—traditional or newer—have I used to make sense of my world or to gain power over my world?

Large Group Exercise:
RACIAL DIFFERENCE and VALUE

Approximate time: one class session

In this exercise, participants examine the racial differences that exist among human beings and the values assigned to those differences by both traditional and new constructs of race.

SUPPLIES: Chalkboard and chalk or poster paper and marking pens.

STUDENT LEADERSHIP: One student volunteers to be the recorder for this exercise.

TO BEGIN: The recorder writes the words RACIAL DIFFERENCE and VALUE at the head of two different columns on the chalkboard or poster paper.

Participants suggest words or phrases that express the racial differences that they have observed among human beings. The recorder writes these words and phrases in the RACIAL DIFFERENCE column.

Participants suggest words or phrases that express the values that they have observed being assigned to these differences. The recorder writes these words and phrases in the VALUE column.

QUESTIONS FOR REFLECTION AND LARGE GROUP DISCUSSION

- What differences do I see among persons of different races and ethnic backgrounds?
- What values do I assign to those differences?
- What surprised me about this exercise?

Racism

Approximate time: two to three class sessions

Racism is a mid-20th-century term that refers to both the belief that different races of people possess either superior or inferior abilities and the practices of discrimination and violence based on that belief (*New Shorter Oxford English Dictionary*, 1993). Joseph Barndt

(1991) has defined three categories of racism: *individual racism,* the prejudices held by a particular person; *cultural racism,* the prejudices held by members of a particular culture or community, and *institutional racism,* a system of economic and social discrimination against racial minorities. Barndt calls institutional racism "prejudice plus power" (p. 28).

In individual racism, persons believe and act on constructs of race learned from their communities. Barndt (1991) likens racist ideas received through language, cultural symbols, and mass media to a tape playing in the mind, reinforcing stereotypes and racial myths in individual attitudes. Both individuals who identify themselves as white and individuals who identify themselves as persons of color can internalize—take within themselves—racist constructs. One striking example of individual racism raised during our pilot program Dealing With Prejudice was that of one student's kindergarten teacher, who had refused to let the black children in her class take naps on the cots in the classroom. "Did she think that our blackness would rub off on the sheets?" the student asked bitterly, nine years later, indicating the depth of her hurt at the teacher's perception of her inferiority.

Cultural racism is built on the construct of the superiority of whiteness and of European cultures. Barndt (1991) points out that non-Western cultures receive little attention in school textbooks, and he claims that the traditional historical notion of the United States as a melting pot further devalues these cultures. Linked to the superiority of whiteness are the social and economic privileges that being white entails. What is called *reverse racism* on the part of persons of color stems from resentment of the unfairness of the privilege and power granted to people who are or who seem white.

Barndt (1991) asserts that many individuals are unconscious of white privilege because of a process of socialization whereby they are isolated from persons of color, numbed to the suffering that racism causes, and conditioned to accept a position of superiority and dominance. Milton Kleg (1993) links racism to an ancient sense of distrust and dislike of outsiders, "those who do not look, speak, or behave as we do" (p. 65).

The creation of racial classifications by 18th-century European scientists, discussed earlier in this chapter, is one example of cultural racism. These classifications legitimized and reinforced beliefs in the superiority of whiteness for generations of Europeans and non-Europeans alike. White supremacist groups today produce literature, videos, and speeches in which people of color, along with Jews and homosexuals, still are portrayed as inferior and even nonhuman (Kleg, 1993). "Learning from the past, we need to remain critically vigilant," bell hooks (1994) says, "willing to interrogate our work as well as our habits of being to ensure that we are not perpetuating internalized racism" (p. 182).

Institutional racism refers to racial inequities that are deeply entrenched in the social and economic systems of the United States. In a country built on the myth of individual success, as discussed in Chapter 3, it is often hard to recognize institutional racism, to understand how an individual's life is influenced by the social and economic system in which he or she lives.

Barndt (1991) defines two levels of institutional racism: *racism in personnel* and *racism in policy and practice*. "Statistical discrimination" (Mickelson, Smith, & Oliver, 1993, p. 23), a term used by sociologists to refer to the practice of employers relying on stereotypes of race and gender when making hiring decisions, is an example of racism in personnel. If an employer relies on racist stereotypes—that a worker who is a person of color may not be reliable, hard working, or competent—then he or she is not likely to hire that person. The continued segregation of Americans, both at work and at home, by race, class, and gender is seen as a major factor in employment discrimination (Mickelson et al., 1993).

Examples of racism in policy and practice (Barndt, 1991) include the lack of representation of persons of color in administrative and leadership roles in a community. A school with no minority principals or assistant principals, a company with no minority executives, a city government with no minority officials are examples of racism in practice.

Derrick Bell (1992) asserts that racism continues in the United States today because it benefits those who have the most stake in the current social and economic system, the 10% of Americans who control 71% of the wealth and wield a great deal of social power (see discussion in Chapter 3). Bell explains his theory in two ways. First, racism provides a justification for the fact that a significant percentage of the African-American population continues to be poor. Second, racism helps to focus the resentments of struggling and poor Americans of all races—the bottom 90% of the population—away from wealthy Americans and onto struggling and poor African-Americans, putting the responsibility for poverty on the poor.

In 1990, 32% of the black population lived in households whose annual income was less than $13,400 a year for a family of four, or below the government-defined poverty line. Eleven percent of the white population lived in households whose annual income was below the poverty line (Farley, 1993).

The continuing poverty gap between black and white Americans is demonstrated in Figure 4.1. This figure shows that although there are wealthy black households and poor white households, since the 1960s white households in the United States have held four to five times the *average* amount of wealth held by black households. This ratio that has not changed despite the increases in the amount of wealth for both black and white households (Mishel & Bernstein, 1994).

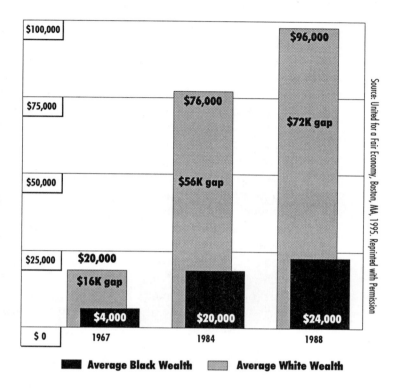

Figure 4.1. Gains and Gaps in Racial Wealth Accumulation
SOURCE: United for a Fair Economy, Boston, MA (1995). Reprinted with permission.

QUESTIONS FOR REFLECTION AND LARGE GROUP DISCUSSION

- What lived experience do I have with individual racism?
- What lived experience do I have with cultural racism?
- What lived experience do I have with institutional racism?
- What relationships do I see between racism and other prejudices?

Individual Exercise: Media Images of Race

Approximate time: one to two class sessions

What cultural images of race exist in the mass media—newspapers, magazines, books, movies, television, music? Do these images portray traditional constructs of race? New constructs of race? Both traditional and new constructs of race?

In this exercise, participants can choose to do one, two, or all three of the following out-of-class assignments to explore the ways in which race is portrayed in our society.

OPTION A: Select one image (photograph, advertisement, illustration, political cartoon) that expresses something you find significant about race or the constructs of race discussed in this chapter. Prepare a brief oral or written reflection on the image to share in class.

OPTION B: Watch television over the course of a week and note how white persons and persons of color are portrayed in commercials, drama shows, comedy shows, and documentaries or news broadcasts. Prepare a brief oral or written report to share in class.

OPTION C: Review a fairy tale or other children's story and note how it portrays white persons and persons of color. Prepare a brief oral or written report to share in class.

In the next class or classes, each participant needs to have the opportunity to share his or her report, although not everyone may choose to speak. After the sharing of reports is completed, the participants may choose to make a collage or display of their images and reports in the classroom or in another area of the school.

QUESTIONS FOR REFLECTION AND LARGE GROUP DISCUSSION

- What constructs of race are displayed by the medium I chose to report on (image, television programs, fairy tale or children's story)?

- How are the constructs I discovered similar to the constructs discovered by other participants?

- How are the constructs I discovered different from those discovered by other participants?

- What surprised me about this exercise?

Individual Exercise: Reading and Reflection— "Coping With Racism"

Approximate time: two class sessions

Before the next class session, the participants read "Coping With Racism," a chapter from *"I Am Who I Am": Speaking Out About Multiracial Identity* by Kathlyn Gay. Because this piece is lengthy, the participants may want to read it to themselves, although they may read it aloud in class (or sign it, using American Sign Language).

The participants prepare reflections on the reading in a form that displays one or more of their multiple intelligences (see Chapter 2)—an essay, a poem, a rap, a song, a dance, a drawing, an equation, a journal entry, a video, or an image. These reflections may be used in group exhibits or displays, in presentations or assemblies, or in individual portfolios.

In preparing their reflections, participants keep in mind the following questions:

QUESTIONS FOR READING AND REFLECTION

- What emotions did this reading evoke in me?
- What lived experience (mine or someone else's) did this reading make me remember?
- What did the reading tell me that I already know and think is important?
- What did the reading tell me that I didn't know and want to know more about?

In the next class sessions, the participants volunteer to share their reflections. Every participant should have a chance to share his or her reflection, although not every participant may choose to do so.

Coping With Racism*

Kathlyn Gay

Kathlyn Gay, who lives in Elkhart, Indiana, is an award-winning writer of books on social and scientific issues for young people.

---

*Kathlyn Gay, "Coping With Racism" from *"I Am Who I Am": Speaking Out About Multiracial Identity*. New York: Franklin Watts. © 1995 by Kathlyn Gay. All rights reserved. Reprinted with permission.

She considers writing an essential form of communication that allows her as a shy person to exercise the gift of walking in another person's shoes.

> It is not easy to be part Red, part White and part Black; part oppressed and part oppressor; part have and part have-not. I feel . . . the primitive struggle between love and hate, us and them, same and different, acceptance and rejection, pluralism and racism.

—*Linda J. Mahdesian, "I Am America," Melange (September 1989), p. 3*

When Allison Joseph, a Vassar College student, was still in high school, she wanted to find out how people of racially mixed ancestry similar to her own coped with prejudicial attitudes and behaviors. Joseph explained: "My father is white, descended from Russian Jews who lived in an area invaded long ago by Asian peoples. Judging by the shape of my father's eyes, his ancestors may have had interactions with the Mongols or others of Asian heritage. His mother is German-Jewish. My mother is black and her family is also mixed: there are Native Americans, Arawak Indians, African Americans and western Europeans in her background."

Joseph reported that her mixed ancestry has prompted only a few prejudicial incidents, which in her opinion, might be due to the fact that she appears "white." As an honors project at Bronx High School of Science in New York, Joseph developed and conducted a study entitled "The Effects of Racism on White-Appearing Children of Integrated Marriages." For her study, described in a 1992 issue of *Interrace* magazine, she interviewed ten young people of mixed ancestry, aged fifteen to twenty, who reported a variety of reactions from classmates and others.

Several girls said that boys found them attractive because of their "exotic" or "interesting" looks. Most respondents said their mixed backgrounds evoked "surprise and sometimes suspicion" from their peers. One teenager felt that her biraciality created tension between herself and others of a single racial background; she thought that people went out of their way not to offend her with racist remarks. Nearly all of the respondents in Joseph's study had experienced some form of discrimination or prejudicial comments. Three respondents said they "consistently experienced discrimination when in public with their darker-skinned parent." But all had learned to cope, which in Joseph's words, "is necessary to avoid getting hurt by racist behaviors."[1]

Helping Young People Cope

Learning to cope is not always a simple matter, however, since some people encounter racist acts that include name-calling, teasing, taunts, and threats of violence against them. Ideally, young people of mixed ancestry have parents who help them combat abuse from those who disapprove of their blended heritage. Such parents are advocates for their children, finding ways to help their offspring gain self-esteem and to be proud of their racially mixed heritage. The parents also work with schools and teachers to combat prejudice about their children's mixed ancestry.

In a study of forty-four young adults of black/white heritage in California, clinical psychologist Agneta Mitchell found that those who identified themselves as biracial had a strong sense of who they were. They felt "they belonged in both worlds" rather than just to one racial group or to no group at all. Mitchell reported that many of the biracial adults had experienced anxiety due to "a lot of stuff from teachers and kids"—put-downs, teasing, and harassment. But, according to Mitchell, once the biracial young people in her study "got through the stress" they became "really healthy" individuals.[2]

If some multiracial individuals, like people of any other group, are unable to get "through the stress" of daily living, they may seek help in counseling. Levonne Gaddy, a psychotherapist, works with such young people. Gaddy helped found Multiracial Americans of Southern California, a support network, and she also helped develop the Center for Interracial Counseling and Psychotherapy in Los Angeles.

Gaddy, who is of African, Cherokee, and European ancestry, attended all-black schools when she was growing up in North Carolina but was constantly teased and harassed because of her light skin color, hair, and gray-green eyes. She said she always "felt different" but considered herself a black person and no one could tell her otherwise. But that identity changed when she went to an all-black college in North Carolina. As she explained:

> During that time I went with a friend to a Black Muslim temple and heard the minister talk about ugly, blue-eyed devils. Even though I identified as black, I knew the minister was talking about part of me. I sank lower and lower in my seat as the minister talked on and on about the evils of white people. The minister then looked over the audience and said: "Fear not, all you light people out there. Your whiteness was raped into you." That was a turning point for me, because I knew that my whiteness had not come from rape and that my white ancestry came from the female side of my family. So from then on I started to examine my own racist attitudes—black against white—and began to acknowledge all of my heritage.[3]

The "Double Whammy"

As pointed out by many of the young people interviewed, one of the problems that people of mixed ancestry may face is hostility from both the dominant and minority groups. At a 1992 meeting of multiracial students at the University of California (UC) Berkeley, a young woman whose mother is of Japanese ancestry (born in Japan) and father is of African heritage (born in the U.S. South), told the group that she is not accepted wholeheartedly by either the Japanese or African-American community. She is often made to feel "different" because "[p]eople think it's so tragic you have to be two things. . . . They just see totality as being one thing. . . . In order to be a whole person, I have to accept both [heritages]."[4]

That is a concept that Terry Wilson, a professor of Native American Studies and Ethnic Studies at UC Berkeley, frequently emphasizes in his classes, particularly in his seminars on "People of Mixed Racial Descent." Wilson explained that his point of view developed because of his own Potawatomi and French-Canadian heritage. He was born on a Kansas Indian reservation but when he was four years old moved with his family to Oklahoma. There he lived with an Indian community of Arapaho and Cheyenne, where he was plagued with taunts about his ancestry.

"In the public school, both white and Indian guys would call me half-breed or just 'breed,' and I'd end up getting right into their faces and beating those faces into a pulp. I'd get into nearly maniacal fights trying to stuff those insults down their throats. My sister and parents always told me that if I ignored the taunts the boys would stop bothering me. But I thought: if I hit the guys enough then they'll stop bothering me!" Wilson said. He explained that his parents did not provide guidance in dealing with mixed-race issues because "it was something people didn't talk about." As a result, he continued fighting over taunts until one day he lost a battle with three boys and ended up in the hospital, battered. He recalled:

> When my father came to visit me in the hospital he told me he was kind of glad I got beat up—not glad I was hurt, but, he said, "You needed to learn that you can't whip everybody and you have to find different ways to deal with the problem" although he didn't say what the problem was! For me it was the beginning of a more balanced way of looking at life. I began to realize that I did have to find different ways to deal with the fact that I was a mixed-race person in a society and culture that does not want to acknowledge my existence.

Wilson's transformation came about during his undergraduate and graduate studies in history, when, he said,

> I learned that people had been lying to me and the books I had been reading about being mixed race, about being a half-breed, had been lying to me. In my study of history, I learned that those persons who were of Indian and white or Indian and black heritage were not unfortunate individuals caught between two cultures with no place to go—as the books said—but just the opposite was the case. Those mixed-race individuals almost to a person were accepted into the various tribal societies and became especially valued members of those societies because they had a huge advantage. They were biracial, bicultural, and bilingual.

As a result, Wilson noted, those of mixed ancestry were able to communicate and deal with people from a variety of cultures. This is a concept that Wilson now passes on to students and others, exhorting individuals of mixed heritage *not* to let everyone else decide who you are but instead to "toughen up and tell them who you are!"[5]

Another Californian of German and Chinese ancestry came to a similar conclusion, but not until she had gone through a great deal of psychological conflict and confusion. Caren (not her real name) and her experiences were described in an academic paper on people of mixed ancestry written by Michelle M. Motoyoshi, who wanted to test the validity of various theories about multiracial individuals. She conducted in-depth interviews with three women, one of whom was Caren.

Motoyoshi explained that Caren attended a "predominantly White elementary school in San Diego, [and] was one of only two people of color in her class . . . She was called 'Chink' and 'Chop Suey' more times than she can or cares to remember. The children, by deriding her, made her feel different, even weird . . ."

Caren also experienced discrimination during her teenage years when she lived in San Francisco's Chinatown. According to Motoyoshi:

> Whites predominated at the school [Caren] attended during the week. There she was ostracized because she was the only Asian around. At Chinese school, on the other hand, she was considered White and was teased because she did not look and could not speak Chinese. As a result . . . Caren viewed herself as an outsider . . . like a misfit.
>
> [She began to associate] primarily with Whites and meticulously emulated their behavior. She lightened her hair. She avoided sunlight for fear of becoming dark-skinned. With the help of lemon juice, she tried to bleach her skin and give herself freckles. Her desperate attempts to be White, however, did not result in her feeling happier or whole, but rather made her even more anxious and self-conscious about her racial background.

After Caren entered college, where she became part of a supportive group of mixed ancestry, she "learned to accept herself and to take pride in who she was," Motoyoshi reported. "[Caren] learned that to be whole, she had to acknowledge she was 'half' and that there was nothing shameful about being so."[6]

Although the other two women Motoyoshi interviewed did not appear to suffer psychological conflicts, they reported being shunned by "cliquish" racial groups and feeling like outsiders at times. But Motoyoshi found that the two women (and others like them) were able to cope with discrimination and the negative messages that society sends about intermixing in part because their families accepted and encouraged multicultural contacts and helped them develop self-esteem.[7]

Elizabeth Atkins, a journalist with the *Detroit News,* is a prime example of a person who has developed coping skills—among them confidence in her own self-worth and a sense of humor—to deal with harassment and discrimination because of her mixed ancestry. In an article for *New People* magazine, she described herself as "a multiracial black woman with long blond hair, green eyes and white-looking skin. With a black mother and white/Native American father, my social and political identities are African-American. But people who judge me on appearance without knowing what I'm all about, especially black women, are angry when they see me with black men. They cut piercing, evil eyes at me, blurt mean comments and whisper angrily to each other while staring at me and my man."

Atkins reported numerous incidents in which she and a male black friend had to deal with the "evil eye" of blacks or ugly insults from whites—"a double whammy of hostility," as she described it. In the past Atkins felt self-conscious about her light skin and upset when black people "couldn't tell that I'm black too." But, she reported, "at age 25, I've finally learned to ignore these incidents or laugh away the pain and anger." In her view the incidents were, and still are

> spawned and fueled by vicious, rampant racism that ravages the black community both externally and internally. From white society, we face racism every day. It gnaws at and corrodes our self-esteem while feeding bitterness and anger toward whites. And among African Americans, a deep-rooted obsession with light skin fosters a self-destructive, stifling and divisive mentality that hinders our political and social agenda . . . this won't change until blacks overcome the belief that white standards of beauty—long hair, light skin and light eyes—are superior to darker skin, kinky hair and broader features. With hope, the emerging Afrocentric pride will remedy that.[8]

Colorism

Atkins' experiences are similar to those described in *"The Color Complex: The Politics of Skin Color Among African Americans,* which explores "colorism," or interracial discrimination based on skin color. The book was initiated by Kathy Russell, who is a "Black woman with fairly light skin and long hair," as she described herself. Russell wanted to investigate the kind of color bias she experienced as an adolescent. Her research led to Midge Wilson, professor of women's studies and psychology at DePaul University in Chicago, and Ronald Hall, assistant professor of social work at Augsburg College in Minneapolis, both of whom had studied the "color complex."

The threesome brought together, in their words: "the perspectives of a Black woman, a White woman, and a Black man on the enormously sensitive topic of skin color and feature discrimination among Blacks." With numerous anecdotes and statistical information, they reveal that

Traditionally, the color complex involved light-skinned Blacks' rejection of Blacks who were darker. Increasingly, however, the color complex shows up in the form of dark-skinned African Americans spurning their lighter-skinned brothers and sisters for not being Black enough. The complex even includes attitudes about hair texture, nose shape, and eye color. In short, the "color complex" is a psychological fixation about color and features that leads Blacks to discriminate against each other. . . . [9]

The origins of "colorism" and color bias in the black community can be traced to the days of slavery, when color coding became part of the racial classification system. During the slave era, light-skinned slaves often were sold for high prices at auctions, and some were even bred for that purpose. Usually light-skinned slaves were household servants, while darker-skinned slaves were relegated to field work and other hard labor. After slavery was abolished, light-skinned blacks frequently gained more privileges than people of darker skin color, and many rose to positions of power. Through the years, light-skinned blacks became an elite group, and the perception developed that light-skinned blacks could advance economically, socially, and politically far easier than those of a darker hue.

According to a 1992 reader poll conducted by *Ebony* magazine, about half of those surveyed still believed that light-skinned blacks were favored, while the other half thought the perception false. The magazine editors cited some evidence to support the perception that light-skinned blacks are more favorably treated than dark-skinned blacks. One example was the "word from many adoption agencies . . . which report that a continuous stream of Black couples—most with mid-brown to dark complexions—express an overwhelming preference for light-complexioned or mixed-race children." Another indicator was a recent study showing that "darker skinned Blacks still face a greater degree of social and economic barriers, with darker skinned Blacks earning sometimes up to 50 percent less than lighter Blacks with similar educational backgrounds and occupational status."[10]

Some people with dark skin try to escape what they view as color bondage. One forty-one-year-old school teacher in Philadelphia explained it this way:

I'm what folks down South call "blue," as in so black, I'm blue. My grandmother told me if I washed myself in milk it would lighten my skin. So that's what I did every day, and I started convincing myself that I was actually getting lighter. I had been raised to believe that skin color, even among black people, really mattered in how you did in school, what job you got, where you lived, who you married and, basically, what kind of life you would have.[11]

In attempts to deal with some of the debilitating effects of negative attitudes about skin color, an increasing number of people are speaking out on color stereotypes. Contemporary black authors such as Alice Walker, Maya Angelou, and Itabari Njeri, and journalists, playwrights, TV script writers, and entertainers have dealt with the subject of colorism in recent years. As the authors of *The Color Complex* stated, they want to help "heal some of the wounds the color issue has inflicted on the African-American community."[12]

The Hawaiian Exception

About the only part of the United States where mixed ancestry is sometimes celebrated is in the state of Hawaii. There mixed ancestry is a well-accepted fact of life. Descendants of Polynesians (who first settled Hawaii), Japanese, Chinese, Korean, Filipino, Portuguese, Europeans, and other groups have learned to share traditions. People of mixed ancestry are now the largest population group in Hawaii.

Hal Glatzer, a journalist for the *San Francisco Chronicle* who worked in Hawaii for eleven years, noted that "After two centuries of living together in close quarters, people in Hawaii . . . know how to relax around people who are different. . . . [Hawaiians] have found it economically, politically or socially unprofitable to be racist."[13]

However, that does not mean Hawaiians have eliminated categories for people. Those who are part Asian and part Caucasian think of themselves and are considered by others to be *hapa heole* (part Caucasian). Those whose heritage may include Asian and Polynesian are known as cosmopolitan or local—not of the mainland. The local category carries with it higher status and "is vastly more important, in social relations, than one's ancestry. Being local implies that one is family centered, concerned with consensus more than accomplishment. . . . Race and ethnicity are trivial compared with the distinction between local and nonlocal," according to sociologist Ronald C. Johnson of the University of Hawaii.[14]

Unfortunately, as is clear from the incidents already described, people of mixed-race ancestry on the U.S. mainland must still struggle with the issues of race and ethnicity. A special 1993 issue of *Time* magazine on "The New Face of America" states:

> During the past two decades, America has produced the greatest variety of hybrid households in the history of the world. As ever increasing numbers of couples crash through racial, ethnic and religious barriers to invent a life together, Americans are being forced to rethink and redefine themselves.[15]

Certainly many people of mixed-race ancestry in the United States are a catalyst in that process, especially when they insist on recognition of their integrated identity and emphasize a shared culture: a diverse and constantly changing American culture.

Source Notes

1. Allison Joseph, "The Effects of Racism on White-Appearing Children of Integrated Marriages," *Interrace* (May-June 1992), pp. 28-32.

2. Quoted in Robert Anthony Watts, "Not Black, Not White, But Biracial Mixed-Race People Questioning Labels," *Atlanta Constitution* (December 1, 1991), p. A1.

3. Comments during "Into the Mix" forum, Berkeley, California, March 13, 1993.

4. Quoted in Dexter Waugh, "Multiracial Students Search for Identity," *San Francisco Examiner* (April 21, 1991), p. B5.

5. From an address by Terry Wilson at the sixth annual Kaleidoscope conference, Los Angeles, CA, October 17, 1992.

6. Michelle M. Motoyoshi, "The Experience of Mixed-Race People: Some Thoughts and Theories," *The Journal of Ethnic Studies,* Summer 1990, pp. 83-84.

7. Ibid., pp. 87-88.

8. Elizabeth Atkins, "If Looks Could Kill," *New People* (September/October 1992), pp. 10-13.

9. Kathy Russell, Midge Wilson, and Ronald Hall, *The Color Complex: The Politics of Skin Color Among African Americans* (New York: Harcourt Brace Jovanovich, 1992), pp. 4-6.

10. "Why Skin Color Suddenly Is a Big Issue Again," *Ebony* (March 1992), pp. 120-121.

11. Quoted in "How Black is Black?" *Boston Globe* (January 19, 1993), Living Section, p. 51.

12. Kathy Russell, Midge Wilson, and Ronald Hall, *The Color Complex: The Politics of Skin Color Among African Americans* (New York: Harcourt Brace Jovanovich, 1992), pp. 166.

13. Hal Glatzer, "The Melting Pot in the Hawaiian Sun," *San Francisco Chronicle* (December 29, 1991), This World section, p. 16Z.

14. Ronald C Johnson, "Offspring of Cross-Race and Cross-Ethnic Marriages in Hawaii," in Maria P. P. Root, ed., *Racially Mixed People in America* (Newbury Park, CA: Sage Publications, 1992), p. 243.

15. Jill Smolowe, "Intermarried . . . with Children," *Time* (special issue, Fall 1993), p. 64.

Large Group Exercise:
Common Ground on Race

Approximate time: one to two class sessions

What concerns do participants have and want to share about issues of race? Common Ground, an exercise adapted from Share the Wealth/United for a Fair Economy in Boston, Massachusetts, is designed to encourage the sharing of thoughts and feelings about a particular issue. As with other exercises in *Dealing With Differences,* Common Ground depends on the participants being respectful of each other and assuming responsibility for the process.

SUPPLIES: Chalkboard and chalk or poster paper and marking pens.

STUDENT LEADERSHIP: Two or more students volunteer to begin the sharing of concerns and to record a summary of concerns and the results of the large group discussion on the chalkboard or poster paper.

TO BEGIN: The participants form a circle. One person then volunteers to be the first to share a concern he or she has about the topic under discussion. This person moves inside the circle and speaks the concern.

Here are some examples of concerns about race taken from our pilot program Dealing With Prejudice:

> I'm concerned because whenever I go into a store in the mall the clerks act like I'm going to steal something, because I'm a black teenager.

> I'm concerned because my friend had to sneak out of the house to meet her boyfriend, who's Indian, because her mother doesn't approve of her seeing him.

> I'm concerned because some people call me "white girl" because I have a light complexion and do well in school.

> I'm concerned because whenever I go into _____ neighborhood, I feel afraid, like I don't belong and that people might do something to me.

Participants who feel that they share the concern expressed—who identify with the speaker because similar things have happened to them or to people they care about—join the speaker inside the circle. These participants can exchange greetings and speak about their identification with the concern if they wish.

After a few minutes, all of these participants move back to the outer circle and another person moves inside the circle to state a concern. This person is joined by the individuals who share his or her concern. After a few minutes of conversation, these participants return to the outer circle.

The process of sharing concerns continues until everyone has had the opportunity to speak, although not everyone may decide to speak.

All participants return to their seats. They take five to ten minutes to summarize the concerns raised in the exercise. An exercise leader writes this summary on the chalkboard or poster paper.

QUESTIONS FOR REFLECTION AND LARGE GROUP DISCUSSION

- Which concerns do I identify or agree with?

- Which concerns do I not identify or agree with?

- How did I feel about the way other participants responded to my concerns?

- What surprised me about this exercise?

Small Group Exercise: Race— Concerns and Suggestions for Action

Approximate time: two class sessions

What concerns about race are most important to the participants? What actions can they take to address these concerns? To explore these questions, in this exercise the participants assemble in the small groups formed in Chapter 2.

Action can take a variety of forms, both individual and collective. It is important that the actions students suggest—however small or incremental—are taken seriously by teachers and administrators and encouraged whenever possible. If teachers dismiss or discourage suggestions for action, students may justly complain that the program is hypocritical or irrelevant to their lives. Here are some examples of actions suggested and taken by students in the pilot program Dealing With Prejudice:

1. Speak up more for yourself and for others in the face of prejudice

2. Form an after-school discussion/action group

3. Go as a class or group to a relevant movie and discuss it afterward

4. Watch as a class or group relevant videos or TV programs

5. Read books and magazines about your concern

6. Write or call the local newspaper, radio station, or TV station about your concern

7. Boycott businesses that ignore or contribute to your concern

8. Meet as a group with school administrators about your concern

9. Volunteer with an existing school, church, or community group that works on your concern

10. Hold a student-run school assembly on your concern

11. Develop a play or presentation on your concern and perform it for the entire school

12. Develop a display or exhibit on your concern in the classroom or elsewhere on school property

SUPPLIES: Poster paper and marking pens.

STUDENT LEADERSHIP: One student in each small group volunteers to record the results of the small group's discussion.

TO BEGIN: Each small group chooses one concern to explore from the list developed and recorded during Common Ground. The group recorder then writes these four column heads:

What do we know (about this concern)?

What do we need to know (about this concern)?

How can we know (about this concern)?

How can we act (on this concern)?

Using as a guideline the principles of critical thinking and I-search described in Chapter 2, each group brainstorms the concern it has chosen. Groups may consult with teachers on completing this process through trips to the school or the public library or calls or meetings with community members. Teachers and students decide together how much I-search can be done during the *Dealing With Differences* sessions and how much can be done outside of class.

When I-search is completed, each small group's recorder summarizes the group's findings on a sheet of poster paper and posts it on the wall to be read and considered by other participants.

Large Group Exercise: Race— Concerns and Suggestions for Action

Approximate time: two class sessions

In this exercise, the participants reflect on the results of the small group discussions and decide which suggestions for action they can implement as individuals, as small groups, or as a class.

SUPPLIES: Chalkboard or chalk or poster paper and marking pens.

STUDENT LEADERSHIP: Two or more students volunteer to give instructions for the exercise and to record the results of the large group discussion.

TO BEGIN: The exercise leaders ask the participants to leave their desks to read the posted results of each small group's discussion. Participants are encouraged to ask questions of one another and to make notes on what they find interesting.

After 10 to 20 minutes of mingling, the participants return to their seats for discussion.

QUESTIONS FOR REFLECTION AND LARGE GROUP DISCUSSION

- Now that I have reviewed all of the suggestions for action, what suggestions would I most like to implement?

- Are these actions I can take as an individual? As part of a group? As a member of this class?

- What help do I need from other participants (students and teachers) in order to take action?

- What help do I need from people outside the classroom (administrators, community members, family) in order to take action?

Guest Speaker on Race

Approximate time: one to two class sessions

At this point, after the participants have discussed race, racism, concerns, and suggestions for action, we recommend that they invite a guest into the classroom to engage in a dialogue with the participants on issues of race. We recommend that the speaker be someone who not only works on issues of race but also has lived experience with these issues. It would be significant if the speaker were a friend or family member of one of the participants.

Local social service organizations; university or college departments of black, African, or multicultural studies; and advocacy organizations such as the Urban League and the NAACP may be able to provide or to recommend speakers.

Racism and Xenophobia

Approximate time: two class sessions

A little-discussed form of prejudice related to but not identical to racism is *xenophobia.* Xenophobia (from the Greek words *xeno,* meaning stranger or foreigner, and *phobia,* meaning fear) is an early-20th-century term that means hatred or dislike of foreigners (*New Shorter Oxford English Dictionary,* 1993). Milton Kleg (1993) relates xenophobia to a fundamental fear of difference that can result in cultural shock, a situation of being uncomfortable among individuals of another culture.

Andrew Hacker (1992) claims that a central question of U.S. life is not who is white, but who may be *considered* white. Immigrants whose children or grandchildren are now considered white once suffered from the effects of xenophobia (Kleg, 1993). At the time that the term xenophobia came into popular use, Americans born in the United States were concerned about large numbers of Eastern and Southern Europeans—among them Italians, Poles, Russians, and Lithuanians—immigrating to the United States. Articles and cartoons of the time portrayed these immigrants as rats and insects swarming over U.S. shores. There was widespread fear that they were inferior and diseased (Kraut, 1994).

In addition to the fear of inferiority and disease, fear of the foreign languages and customs that the immigrants brought with them fueled xenophobia. It was also fueled by economic fears—fears that the immigrants would take jobs away from Americans born in the United States and that they would receive special services from the government.

In response to these fears, the U.S. government enacted a quota system in 1924 that froze immigration to the United States at low levels. The precedent for this law was set by laws enacted in 1882 and 1908 to restrict the numbers of Chinese immigrants to the United States (Allport, 1954/1979).

Immigration and xenophobia remain important issues in U.S. life. Americans born in the United States of all races are concerned about illegal immigration, benefits and jobs received by immigrants, and tensions between immigrants and Americans born in the United States. Immigrants of all races still suffer from prejudice and pressure to assimilate—to join to the American way of life—adopting the English language, U.S. clothes, and U.S. customs.

QUESTIONS FOR REFLECTION AND LARGE GROUP DISCUSSION

- What lived experience do I have with xenophobia?

- What lived experience did my relatives or ancestors have with xenophobia?

- What relationships do I see between xenophobia and racism? Between xenophobia and other prejudices?

Individual Exercise: Reading and Reflection— "Racism Doesn't Grow Up"

Approximate time: two class sessions

Before the next class sessions, the participants read "Racism Doesn't Grow Up" by Joyce Lee. This essay may be read aloud in class (or signed, using American Sign Language) if participants feel that doing so would deepen their responses to it.

The participants prepare reflections on the essay in a form that displays one or more of their multiple intelligences (see Chapter 2)—an essay, a poem, a rap, a song, a dance, a drawing, an equation, a journal entry, a video, or an image. The reflections may be used in group exhibits or displays, in presentations or assemblies, or in individual portfolios.

In preparing their reflections, participants keep in mind the following questions:

QUESTIONS FOR READING AND REFLECTION

- What emotions did this reading evoke in me?

- What lived experience (mine or someone else's) did this reading make me remember?

- What did the reading tell me that I already know and think is important?

- What did the reading tell me that I didn't know and want to know more about?

In the next class sessions, the participants volunteer to share their reflections. Every participant should have a chance to share his or her reflection, although not every participant may choose to do so.

Racism Doesn't Grow Up*

Joyce Lee

Joyce Lee is an award-winning independent filmmaker living in San Francisco. She is interested in film as a medium for expressing cultural diversity and understanding among the many various immigrant cultures living in America. Currently, she is in preproduction for a documentary on racism with the same title as the following essay.

I came to Portland, Oregon, in 1969 from Hong Kong. I came with my mother and my two brothers, and was placed in school almost immediately after I arrived. I was in a K-5 school in a working-class neighborhood, where I experienced the pain of racism firsthand. I remember in kindergarten, standing next to the bathroom, in front of the children's coat rack, immobile, for an entire school year. I had no friends and didn't talk with anyone, including the teachers. After a few months, the teachers didn't talk to me either. We just coexisted in the room, me with the coat racks, the other children with the teachers. If a classmate gave me any attention, I stood as still as possible, wanting him or her to think I wasn't a real person. I was glad to be an inanimate object. Eventually the classmate would lose interest. It got to be an understanding between myself and the class. They would treat me like a statue and I would behave like one. Actually, they treated me better than a statue; I didn't get vandalized. And, because I was a statue tucked away in the corner, I was never in anyone's way. I didn't make noise and tried not to blink or move. I was actually content with the arrangement. I was even more content to stay home but ended up in school every day for no reason I could see.

I don't remember what happened at the end of the day. I think my mother must have come by to pick me up. When I saw her, I was human again.

If I had to use the bathroom, I waited until I thought no one was looking, used it as fast as possible, and returned to my corner.

It must have been frustrating for kindergarten teachers to have me in their class. They were probably at a loss as to what to do, since I didn't respond or participate. They decided that I was mentally retarded. My mother, who spoke no English, was told that I would be enrolled in a school for retarded children. She was horrified, but she couldn't convince my teachers that I

---

*Joyce Lee, "Racism Doesn't Grow Up" from E. Featherston (Ed.), *Skin Deep: Women Writing on Color, Culture and Identity*. Freedom, California: Crossing Press. © 1994 Joyce Lee. Reprinted with permission. This essay incorporates changes made by the author for republication.

was normal. My aunt, who did speak English, couldn't convince them either.

Out of ingenuity and desperation, my mother told me to fold lots of paper boats and birds in school. She taught me every paper boat she knew, every bird, frog, pig, and so on. (I already knew how to fold some boats. Paper boat races are common among little children in Hong Kong.) When I displayed my origami skills at school, I was no longer categorized as a "special child."

What happened after this time is a little fuzzy. I remember that there was a different attitude toward me. The other kids didn't think I was dumb anymore. I still didn't talk, but eventually a special effort was made to integrate me into activities, an effort to which I responded. There was also a special effort to teach me English, which I had not understood before. When I grasped some of the language, I started to excel.

Looking back, I try to understand why I refused to budge from my spot. I suspect that I distrusted everyone. With the exception of one American-born Chinese girl who spoke English, no one else looked like me. I also didn't understand the language and the interactions between teacher and student. In Hong Kong, corporal punishment and abuse were common at school. Writing the Chinese character "father" wrong meant a couple of slaps on the hand and face. If you persisted in writing the character wrong, you would lose bathroom privileges or lunch privileges. That was in a nursery school. The Oregon kindergarten teachers, by contrast, didn't discipline the children. I didn't trust them.

Whoopi Goldberg has a stand-up routine in which she plays a little Black girl who wears a mop on her head because she wants to be White. As I was growing up, I wanted to be White too. After third grade the kids became meaner. When kids made fun of me in second or first grade, I didn't know enough of the language to be offended or hurt. After third grade, I knew a lot of English. The treatment seemed to get worse. "Chink," "slanty eyes," "Jap," "Hong Kong phooey" were names I grew up with. When I wasn't called those names, I was sometimes beaten up after school by one or two kids waiting for me. Surprisingly, I was beaten up not just by White kids, but also Black kids. In fact, the Black kids were worse than the White ones. The White ones would take me on singularly, but the Black kids were often in groups. When I reached high school, the racism continued—although I didn't get beaten up anymore.

By high school, White kids and Black kids segregated, they had little to do with each other, except in school sports. The racial hatred I experienced was from the football jocks, not the jocks who were from educated middle-class families, but primarily jocks from poor blue-collar families. There were quite a few of these guys. Some of the girls on the cheerleading team, from middle-class families, also showed their contempt for non-Whites.

My school had huge racial and economic class gaps. We had a program for Asian refugees from Cambodia, Vietnam, and

Laos. We also had a program for juvenile delinquents, who had a choice of attending institutions or attending my high school. On the other side of the spectrum, we had programs for young scholars who were too advanced in certain subjects to continue high school and had the option of attending Reed College for a few courses on scholarship. With this ethnic, academic, and class diversity, one might have expected a little more sophistication, more tolerance. Unfortunately, this was not the case.

The refugees were hated and often targets of racial violence. Sometimes, I would see other Chinese students get threatened and harassed. I felt sorry for them but at the same time relieved that, for the moment, it wasn't me. I hated myself for a long time and was ashamed of being Chinese, was ashamed of being an immigrant with uneducated parents, ashamed of being poor. For thirteen years, I endured a constant barrage of racial slurs.

I remember one incident that was particularly harrowing. During one of our annual picnics in the park, the varsity football rednecks decided that the picnic was being "invaded by gooks" and started bashing heads for recreation. The Asian refugees, probably tired of being picked on day after day, fought back for a change. The fight turned into a race riot involving two hundred students. I avoided a pummeling that day by running out of the park as fast as I could.

Even though I was on the school paper and art staff, I was still regarded as a "gook." I had hoped that, all the years I had endured these rednecks had built me some kind of immunity. I was an active student, a student who had something to contribute on *their* terms. I was a senior at that time and had distinguished myself from the refugees, primarily to show that I wasn't like them. I was really "American."

My high school wasn't too different from any other high school in America, nor were my experiences particularly special. I know I had it better than most immigrants in this country.

What I find incredible after all these years is not the racism I encountered, or even the violence and hatred against my people, but the institutional blind eye to that racism. The educators, school administrators, and parents of those jocks did *nothing* about the racial problems at our school. Instead, the race riot in the park was hushed up. There was no discussion of what happened. After the riot, it was just another day.

Today, in San Francisco, I run into an occasional racial slur—although not to the extent I did when I was younger. The so-called "Asian invasion" is the label attached to Asians who are able to accomplish the same goals that Euro-immigrants accomplish. I've encountered a few resentful Whites. However, most of the damage from my childhood manifests itself in more internal ways.

Feelings of insignificance, of low self-esteem, are qualities acquired from a childhood in America. Feelings of inadequacy creep up when I date a White guy; guilt accompanies us to a movie or restaurant. I'm paranoid that all White women secretly hate me. I feel inadequate around educated White middle-class people in a social setting. I compensate by putting on a confidence mask. "Oh, yes, I am educated, too, and I grew up in a mainstream family. Oh, yes, we celebrate Christmas, of course—my family lives in the suburbs." I feel stupid when this happens because my conformity is transparent. The confidence mask is thin.

I would be kidding myself if I didn't acknowledge some Westernization and assimilation into American culture. My family calls me "banana," yellow outside, white inside. English is now my "first language." I spend little time in Chinatown, and don't get to speak Chinese that often. This doesn't mean that I'm not proud of my heritage and that I've embraced Western values 100 percent. I'm part of that culture that has rejected mainstream options like marriage, kids, house, security, suburbia—options available in both in my cultures: American and Chinese.

To totally embrace Chinese values is very similar to a total embrace of American values: marriage, kids, hard work, steady income, house in suburbia, television, and a set of "practical" goals. The obligation that is not part of the Western model is lifelong obligation and duty to elders. No thank you.

The greatest agony for me, even after those years in Oregon, is discovering how little things have changed. It's been approximately fifteen years since I was entrapped in the Portland Public School System. The other day my little eleven-year-old cousin, who arrived from China two years ago, took me aside and revealed to me the shame she was facing in school. "There are things I don't tell my parents," she said. Reluctantly, she told me how the White kids at school picked on her, said mean, racist things to her, pushed her around. Since she barely spoke English, she had a hard time making friends; she dreads school.

What consoling words did I have for her? All I could say to her was, "It's not you, it's never you, it's their stupidity/ignorance. Unfortunately, there're a lot of them, and only one of you. Just remember, I'll be there if you need to talk to me anytime." I didn't have the heart to tell her what to expect in high school. I did tell her that I went through the same things she did. I felt helpless; I couldn't offer her any more than those few scant sentences.

5

Gender, Sexism, and Heterosexism

*My cousin . . . when he has friends
over . . . they always say how cute I am,
and stuff. . . . I don't like hearing that. Just
because I'm a girl doesn't mean I want to
do this and that with you. You know, I
don't even know you. . . . You know,
you're walking down the street, and guys
say this and that. That doesn't make me
feel cute. . . . I tell them I'm a woman. I'm
a female. I'm not, you know, your toy.*

—student from pilot program Dealing With Prejudice

Gender *has been defined since the mid-20th century as referring to
the differences between men and women that arise not from biology
but from society and culture (New Shorter Oxford English Dictionary, 1993). In the United States today, new definitions of gender
are being developed by those who question traditional distinctions
between male and female gender roles (Friend, 1993; hooks, 1994).
New definitions of gender also take into account the persistence of
gender prejudice and violence (Friend, 1993; Harris & Associates,
1994; Sadker & Sadker, 1994), and the sense of gender as a source*

of personal identity, community, and pride, particularly for women, gay men, and lesbians (Fricke, 1981; Orenstein, 1994).

Using the exercises, discussion topics, and readings in this chapter, participants will explore their own ideas and feelings about gender and difference; the construction of gender; sexism, homophobia, and heterosexism and their relationships to other prejudices; individual experiences with gender; and suggestions for action on gender issues in the classroom and community.

This chapter contains the following sections. The times given to complete them are approximate.

Icebreaker: "The Gift" (one to two class sessions)
What Is Gender? (two class sessions)
Large Group Exercise: MASCULINE/VALUE and FEMININE/ VALUE (one class session)
Sexism (two to three class sessions)
Individual Exercise: Media Images of Gender (one to two class sessions)
Heterosexism and Homophobia (two class sessions)
Individual Exercise: Reading and Reflection—"Reflections of a Rock Lobster" (two class sessions)
Large Group Exercise: Common Ground on Gender (one to two class sessions)
Small Group Exercise: Gender—Concerns and Suggestions for Action (two class sessions)
Large Group Exercise: Gender—Concerns and Suggestions for Action (two class sessions)
Guest Speaker on Gender (one to two class sessions)
Gender and Self-Esteem in School (two class sessions)
Individual Exercise: Reading and Reflection—"One Sister's Love of Beauty" (two class sessions)

Icebreaker: "The Gift"

Approximate time: one to two class sessions

How do individuals define the appropriate interests and behaviors for a boy? For a girl? How do ideas and feelings about the differences and similarities between boys and girls—and between men and women—influence identity?

In the exercise "The Gift," participants examine these questions through the subject of toys, a primary way in which boys and girls learn the business of life, the kind of work that they will do when they are men and women (Freeman & Freeman, 1962). As with other exercises in *Dealing With Differences,* "The Gift" depends on the participants being respectful of each other and assuming responsibility for the process.

SUPPLIES: Chalkboard and chalk or poster paper and marking pens; blue, pink, and yellow construction paper; scissors; toys (baby doll, Barbie™ doll, stuffed animal, toy gun, action toy such as a Power Ranger,™ and other toys suggested by exercise leaders). If toys are not available, exercise leaders can substitute poster paper with the names of toys written on them.

STUDENT LEADERSHIP: Two or more students volunteer to help to prepare the supplies for this exercise, to give instructions, and to record the results of the large group discussion on the chalkboard or poster paper.

PREPARATION (done before class): The exercise leaders bring to the classroom the toys that will be used during the icebreaker. They also cut blue, pink, and yellow construction paper into pieces large enough to be seen throughout the classroom (each participant will receive one blue, one pink, and one yellow piece of paper) and write the following list of toys on the chalkboard or on poster paper.

LIST OF TOYS:
    Barbie™ doll
    football
    computer
    Sega Genesis™
    picture book
    mountain bike
    baby doll
    play stove and microwave
    jump rope
    Barney™ videos
    gym set with swings and slide
    paint set
    play lawn mower
    baseball bat, glove, and ball
    play doctor's kit
    play nurse's kit
    Lion King™ stuffed animal
    toy gun
    My Buddy™ doll
    Power Ranger™

TO BEGIN: The exercise leaders ask the participants to move their desks into a large circle or semicircle. The exercise leaders then pass out the pieces of colored construction paper, instructing the participants that when the name of each toy is called out, they are to use the different colors of paper to express whether they would give the toy in question to a boy, to a girl, or to either a girl or a boy.

If a participant feels that he or she would give the toy only to a girl, the participant raises the pink paper. If a participant feels that he or she would give the toy only to a boy, the participant raises the blue paper. If the participant feels that he or she would give the toy to either a boy or a girl, the participant raises the yellow paper.

The exercise leaders call out the names of the toys and the participants raise their papers. As the names of the toys are called out, the recorder counts the number of blue, pink, and yellow papers raised and puts a tally next to the toy's name.

The exercise leaders then pass the actual toys (or the pieces of poster paper with the names of toys) around the circle. As a toy is passed around the circle, the exercise leaders ask participants to think carefully about the toy and their lived experience with it.

After this process is completed, the participants engage in discussion.

QUESTIONS FOR REFLECTION AND LARGE GROUP DISCUSSION

- What toy or toys would I give only to a girl? Only to a boy? To either a girl or a boy? Why?
- What toys did I play with as a young child? Why?
- What toys did I not play with as a young child? Why?
- What surprised me about this exercise?

What Is Gender?

Approximate time: two class sessions

In its modern sense, *gender* does not refer to the biological differences between boys and girls that exist at birth or to the biological differences that exist between men and women—although biological differences, such as the fact that women bear children, influence ideas about gender. Gender refers instead to the social behaviors that determine what it is to be a man or a woman, to be masculine or feminine.

Used in this way, gender is a *construct,* a social concept or idea. Constructs about gender—as about class, race, and disability—help individuals and groups to make sense of their world as well as to gain social and economic control of their world. The key to the construction of gender—as of race (see Chapter 4) and class (see Chapter 3)— is not the physical or cultural differences that exist between individuals but the ways in which value is assigned to these differences (Rothenberg, 1992). Acknowledging difference is merely saying that X is different from Y; assigning value to difference is saying that X is superior or inferior to Y.

Children become aware of gender constructs at an early age. Although both boys and girls may be active and aggressive in play, a young boy is more likely to pretend to be Superman than a young girl, who might instead pretend to be Wonder Woman. Girls who wear pants are likely to be perceived by other children as more masculine and as enjoying activities such as climbing trees, whereas girls who wear skirts are likely to be perceived as more feminine and as enjoying activities such as playing with dolls (Kaiser, 1990).

A child may be discouraged from a certain type of toy or game because gender constructs have led the child, or the child's parents or teachers, to think of the toy or game as inappropriate—sissy or tomboyish—even if it is enjoyable and useful (Freeman & Freeman, 1962). Playing with dolls may be considered a sissy activity for a boy, for example, although many boys grow up to be fathers of children whom they bathe, sing to, feed, and change, tasks that can be learned in part by playing with dolls (hooks, 1984).

Traditional concepts of gender rely on the "'domestic code,' under which home or family becomes defined as women's place, and a public sphere of power and work as men's place" (Weis, 1993, p. 247). The domestic code persists in spite of the fact that many women have worked and continue to work outside the home. It is fed by the "ideology of romance" (McRobbie, 1978; Valli, 1986) in which women are encouraged to find fulfillment primarily in their personal, home, and family lives and only secondarily in their work lives.

Today, traditional concepts of gender coexist and conflict with new concepts of gender that encourage women to achieve in the public sphere and to consider themselves strong, independent be-ings, and encourage men to become more nurturing and more involved with their personal, home, and family lives. In a study of young men and women at a high school in a neighborhood where people were struggling economically, Lois Weis (1993) found that the young men talked about establishing homes in which they would have traditional control over their wives and children. The young women, on the other hand, talked about getting higher education and jobs, and postponing marriage and children until they were 30 years old.

In a study of the popularity of romance novels among young women at three different middle schools in the Midwest, Linda K. Christian-Smith (1993) discovered a "tug of war between femininity and more assertive modes" (p. 183). These young women from a variety of class and racial backgrounds preferred books in which the men were sensitive and the women stood up for themselves, finding paying work when necessary. The books, however, usually ended with the heroine becoming wealthy, married, and a mother, a "*Horatia* Alger fantasy" (p. 186) that joins traditional constructs of gender with traditional constructs of class.

QUESTIONS FOR REFLECTION AND LARGE GROUP DISCUSSION

- Who and what has influenced my thoughts and feelings about gender?

- How has gender influenced who I am and who I want to be?

- What constructs of gender—traditional or new—have I used to make sense of my world or to gain power over my world?

Large Group Exercise: MASCULINE/VALUE and FEMININE/VALUE

Approximate time: one class session

In this exercise, participants examine their ideas about the differences between *masculine* and *feminine,* and the values assigned to those differences by both traditional and new constructs of gender.

SUPPLIES: Chalkboard and chalk or poster paper and marking pens.

STUDENT LEADERSHIP: One student volunteer to be the recorder for this exercise.

TO BEGIN: The recorder writes the phrases MASCULINE/VALUE and FEMININE/VALUE at the head of two different columns on the chalkboard or poster paper.

Participants suggest words or phrases that express the qualities or attributes they define as masculine and the values they associate with those words or phrases. The recorder writes these phrases down in the MASCULINE/VALUE column.

Participants suggest words or phrases that express the qualities or attributes they define as feminine and the values they associate with those words or phrases. The recorder writes these phrases down in the FEMININE/VALUE column.

QUESTIONS FOR REFLECTION AND
LARGE GROUP DISCUSSION

- What do I consider to be masculine? What values do I assign to these differences?

- What do I consider to be feminine? What values do I assign to these differences?

- What do I consider to be neither (or both) masculine nor feminine? What values to I assign to these attributes?

- Which of these values has been influenced by traditional constructs of gender?

- Which of these values has been influenced by newer constructs of gender?

- What surprised me about this exercise?

Sexism

Approximate time: two to three class sessions

Sexism, a term dating from the mid-20th century, refers to both the belief that women are inferior to men and the practices of discrimination and violence based on that belief, although it is occasionally used to refer to its opposite, the belief that men are inferior to women (*New Shorter Oxford English Dictionary,* 1993). The three categories of racism defined in Chapter 4 (Barndt, 1991) can also be applied to sexism: *individual sexism,* the prejudices held by a particular person; *cultural sexism,* the prejudices held by members of a particular culture or community, and *institutional sexism,* systemic economic and social discrimination against women. Institutional sexism, like institutional racism, is "prejudice plus power" (Barndt, 1991, p. 28).

In individual sexism, persons believe in and act on constructs of gender learned from their communities. Both men and women can internalize—take within themselves—sexist constructs. Sexual teasing, harassment, and violence are examples of individual sexism. Girls are more likely to be teased and harassed over their appearance and sexual behavior than boys. Myra and David Sadker (1994) report an incident in a high school classroom they visited in which a girl who spoke out in a class discussion about the sexist behaviors of a group of boys in her school was cursed and threatened by the same boys within a few minutes of leaving the classroom. Incidents of harassment, threat, and even assault have made many school spaces into "hostile hallways" where young women feel neither safe nor respected (Harris & Associates, 1994).

Cultural sexism refers to the beliefs that influence both individuals and groups to behave in sexist ways. The domestic code that places women in the private sphere and men in the public sphere and the ideology of romance that sweetens the arrangement are examples of cultural sexism.

There is a price to be paid when the existence of cultural sexism is glossed over or denied. Lyn Mikel Brown and Carol Gilligan (1992) found in a long-range study of grade school, middle school, and high school girls in Cleveland, Ohio, that some of the most confident and outspoken girls—both white girls and girls of color—lost their voices as they reached the ages of 11, 12, and 13. In *Shortchanging Girls, Shortchanging America* (American Association of University Women [AAUP], 1991), Gilligan attributes this loss of voice among adolescent girls to the fact that just as girls reach an understanding of the unfairness of society, including the unfair treatment of women, their "moment of resistance" (p. 25) is silenced by other people—including teachers and parents—who do not want to listen to their concerns.

Institutional sexism refers to gender inequities that are deeply entrenched in the social and economic systems of the United States. Just as with race and class, there are serious imbalances in the numbers of poor Americans by gender (Wolf, 1992). Twenty-five percent of all women working full-time earn less than $10,000 per year. Many of these women are in low-status jobs traditionally held by women—secretary, preschool teacher, bank teller, and food service worker—for which the average salary is less than $15,000 per year. Even when women are doing the same job as men, however, they often earn less. Female retail salespersons earn on average only 50% of what male retail salespersons earn. Female bus drivers earn on average only 63% of what male bus drivers earn. Overall, women in the United States earn only 54 to 66 cents for every dollar that men earn—a gap that has not changed since the 1970s.

Figure 5.1 breaks down the median weekly earnings of full-time U.S. workers by race and gender for 1994. (*Median* means the midpoint; equal numbers of workers earned wages above and below the median number.) Note that these figures represent the wages of individuals working full-time, not part-time.

The data in Figure 5.1 reflect serious economic inequities by gender and race. On average, all women earn less than all men, white women earn less than white men, black women earn less than black men, and Hispanic women earn less than Hispanic men. On average, black men and women earn less than white men and women, and Hispanic men and women earn less than black men and women.

Median weekly earnings in 1994 ranged from $547 ($28,444 per year) for white men to $305 ($15,860 per year) for Hispanic

Source: U.S. Department of Labor

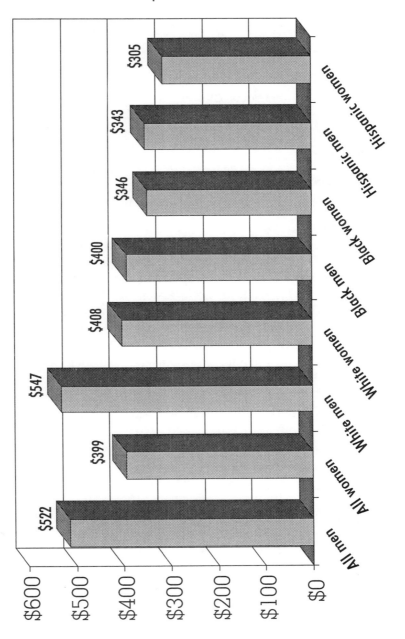

Figure 5.1. Median Weekly Earnings of Full-Time Workers in 1994
SOURCE: U.S. Department of Labor, Bureau of Labor Statistics (1995, p. 207).

87

women. Compare these figures with those for the "good job" defined by Dolbeare and Hubbell (1996; see Chapter 3).

QUESTIONS FOR LARGE GROUP REFLECTION AND DISCUSSION

- What lived experience do I have with individual sexism?
- What lived experience do I have with cultural sexism?
- What lived experience do I have with institutional sexism?
- What relationships do I see between sexism and other prejudices?

Individual Exercise: Media Images of Gender

Approximate time: one to two class sessions

What cultural images of gender exist in the mass media—newspapers, magazines, books, movies, television, music? Do these images portray traditional constructs of gender? Newer constructs of gender? Both traditional and newer constructs of gender?

In this exercise, participants can choose to do one, two, or all three of the following out-of-class assignments to explore the ways in which gender is portrayed in our society.

OPTION A: Select one image (photograph, advertisement, illustration, political cartoon) that expresses something you find significant about men, women, or the constructs of gender discussed in this chapter. Prepare a brief oral or written reflection on the image to share in class.

OPTION B: Watch television over the course of a week and note how men and women are portrayed in commercials, drama shows, comedy shows, and documentaries or news broadcasts. Prepare a brief oral or written report to share in class.

OPTION C: Review a fairy tale or other children's story and note how it portrays men and women. Prepare a brief oral or written report to share in class.

In the next class or classes, each participant needs to have the opportunity to share his or her report, although not everyone may choose to speak. After the sharing of reports is completed, the participants may choose to make a collage or display of their images and reports in the classroom or in another area of the school.

QUESTIONS FOR REFLECTION AND
LARGE GROUP DISCUSSION

- What constructs of gender are displayed by the medium I chose to report on (image, television programs, fairy tale, or children's story)?

- How are the constructs I discovered similar to the constructs discovered by other participants?

- How are the constructs I discovered different from those discovered by other participants?

- What surprised me about this exercise?

Heterosexism and Homophobia

Approximate time: two class sessions

Another meaning of the word *sexism* is the insistence—by an individual, a community, or an institution—that women and men conform to certain constructs of gender, that men be masculine and women feminine. This meaning links sexism to *homophobia (homosexual + phobia,* the Latin word for fear), a mid-20th-century term that means fear of or hostile behavior toward persons who are or who are perceived to be homosexual—bisexual, lesbian, or gay (*New Shorter Oxford English Dictionary,* 1993). White supremacist groups, among others, have made homosexuals targets of violence and hatred (Kleg, 1993).

An even newer term joins the issues of sexism and homophobia more closely. *Heterosexism (hetero + sexism)* is used to refer to the belief that everyone should be or should behave like a heterosexual (Friend, 1987). Heterosexism (Friend, 1993) is cultural and institutional homophobia, whereby individuals are rewarded for being or appearing to be heterosexual and punished for being or appearing to be homosexual. Heterosexism often is supported and reinforced by families. Richard Friend (1993) relates a story of a teenager who, after she revealed to her mother that she was a lesbian, was told by her mother that she was sick and should go to a doctor.

Friend (1993) identifies two ways in which heterosexism is manifested in schools. One is *systematic exclusion,* whereby lesbian, gay, and bisexual people are silenced and their presence ignored or denied both in the classroom and in textbooks. Assigning students to read *The Color Purple* but not allowing them to discuss the lesbian relationship in the book is one example of systematic exclusion. Another way in which heterosexism is manifested in schools is *systematic inclusion,* in which homosexuality is discussed only in negative terms, as a sickness or a danger. Bringing homosexuality into the classroom only in discussions of HIV/AIDS is one example of systematic inclusion.

QUESTIONS FOR REFLECTION AND LARGE GROUP DISCUSSION

- What lived experience do I have with homophobia?

- What lived experience do I have with heterosexism?

- Have I experienced or witnessed systematic exclusion in school?

- Have I experienced or witnessed systematic inclusion in school?

- What relationships do I see between homophobia and heterosexism and other prejudices?

Individual Exercise: Reading and Reflection— "Reflections of a Rock Lobster"

Approximate time: two class sessions

Before the next class session, the participants read "Reflections of a Rock Lobster" by Aaron Fricke. This book excerpt may be read aloud in class (or signed, using American Sign Language) if participants feel that doing so would deepen their responses to it.

The participants prepare reflections on the reading in a form that displays one or more of their multiple intelligences (see Chapter 2)—an essay, a poem, a rap, a song, a dance, a drawing, an equation, a journal entry, a video, or an image. These reflections may be used in group exhibits or displays, in presentations or assemblies, or in individual portfolios.

In preparing their reflections, participants keep in mind the following questions:

QUESTIONS FOR READING AND REFLECTION

- What emotions did this reading evoke in me?

- What lived experience (mine or someone else's) did this reading make me remember?

- What did the reading tell me that I already know and think is important?

- What did the reading tell me that I didn't know and want to know more about?

In the next class sessions, the participants volunteer to share their reflections. Every participant should have a chance to share his or her reflection, although not every participant may choose to do so.

Reflections of a Rock Lobster*

Aaron Fricke

Aaron Fricke was living in Cumberland, Rhode Island, in 1980 when he made national headlines after a federal district court judge ruled that Fricke could bring a male date to his high school prom. With humor and insight, the following book excerpt chronicles Fricke's decision to fight for his rights and his prom night experience.

In April, Mr. Lynch held the traditional pep talk to jolt the graduating class out of senioritis. Just as he had done the previous autumn, he referred to the "problem" that had existed at the 1979 prom. Naturally, the students exploded in enthusiasm. I wanted to stand up and scream, "I am gay and proud and will not be oppressed!" I was determined that Mr. Lynch would not go on forever stirring up this prejudice in the hearts of my fellow students. But for the time, discretion prevailed. Besides, I valued the use of my two legs.

Everyone buzzed about the prom after Mr. Lynch's speech. The girls planned to make or buy their gowns. Some guys reminisced about last year's prom. But like always, I was left out of these discussions. Through all of my high school years I had been left out and I was tired of it. I wanted to be part of the group like all the other students.

The simple, obvious thing would have been to go to the senior prom with a girl. But that would have been a lie—a lie to myself, to the girl, and to all the other students. What I *wanted* to do was to take a male date. But as Paul had shown the year before, such honesty is not always easy.

There was an important difference between Paul's case and mine, though. Paul had not been able to fight for his rights because he was seventeen at the time. I was now eighteen and legally able to make my own decision. If I wanted to go to the prom with a male escort and the school tried to stop me, I could take the case to court.

But should I do that? This would require much thought if I was to make a decision without being selfish, uncaring or irrational.

If I went to the prom with another guy, what would be the benefits? For myself, it would mean participating in an important social event and doing so with a clear conscience and a sense of wholeness. But how would it affect the rest of the people involved?

I believed that those who had themselves faced discrimination or prejudice would immediately understand what I was doing and its implications for human rights. There would be others who may never have had direct experiences with prejudice but who would recognize my right to the date of my choice. These people may have been misled to believe that homosexuality is wrong, but they could still understand that my rights were being denied.

At the opposite end of the spectrum were the homophobics who might react violently. But the example I set would be perfect for everyone. We would be just one more happy couple. Our happiness together would be something kids could relate to. I would be showing that my dignity and value as a human being were not affected by my sexual preference.

I concluded that taking a guy to the prom would be a strong positive statement about the existence of gay people. Any opposition to my case (and I anticipated a good bit) would show the negative side of society—not of homosexuality.

To attend the prom with a girl would not be unenjoyable, but it would be dishonest to my true feelings. Besides, most kids now knew I was gay. If I went with a female, I would probably have received more taunts than from going with a male. By going with a male I would win some respect from the more mature students, and I would keep my self-esteem.

I tried not to worry about the possibility of violence. Certainly I would face opposition. It was inevitable given the rampant prejudice against homosexuals today. But the threat of violence was not enough to change my mind, since I encountered that every day to some degree. Perhaps such threats would diminish in the future as people saw more homosexuals participating openly in everyday life.

My biggest concern was for my parents. Although the entire student body and administration of Cumberland High School knew or assumed I was gay, my family had remained blissfully blind to this reality. The news could be heartbreaking to them. Plus, it might get them ostracized by the neighbors, banned from town social gatherings . . . from church . . . from Tupperware parties! Was I willing to take the risk? No! As much as I believed in my rights, I valued my relationship with my parents too much to have it abruptly severed. After all, for years I had hidden my sexuality for fear of losing my parents' love. As a child it had been *the* most important thing to me. Now, as a man, it was just as important as before. I wanted to go to my prom, but it was not as important as eighteen years of love.

I decided to tell my parents of my homosexuality first, then ask them how they would feel about my going to the prom. If it seemed like too much for them to accept, I would forget the prom and just be happy that I no longer had to be secretive with my parents. But if they rejected me merely because I was gay, then I would still pursue my rights, even at the prom, realizing that my parents were good people but were horribly misled.

Until now, I had never spoken to them about my homosexuality. Like many adolescents I had drifted away from my parents lately. Now I had an impetus to improve my communication with them. I decided to approach my parents separately; a thousand times I rehearsed what I would say.

It began, "Ever since I was a kid . . . " and ended, "I hope you love me enough not to reject me." But when the moment of truth came I felt more self-confident and said, "I don't know if you've had any suspicions, but I'm gay."

Long pause. My mother replied, "I'm so glad you were finally able to be honest with me." She had long suspected. My father had not; when I told him he broke down and cried. Yet they both loved me unconditionally. When I explained why I wanted to go to the prom they were supportive. I was my own man, they each said, and I would have to make my own decisions.

It felt great to be able to talk to my parents about this. Their reaction was encouraging and I decided to go ahead. I would invite Paul Guilbert to the prom.

Anne Guillet wrote me a note in environmental science class when I asked for her advice about the prom. She wrote:

Dear Aaron,

Last year, Paul's attempt to bring a guy to the prom was seen by most people, in fact I think by all, as a grab at publicity. That was because no one knew Paul, he just showed up out of the clear blue sky (and raised a ruckus). Since you've been in Cumberland much longer and have more close friends, people won't suspect you of such ill motives so easily, but this is what they will think.

1. Paul made you do it.
2. You're crazy.
3. You believe in gay rights.

In that order. Now *I* know you did it for reason 3 but you should think about how other people are going to react and I think you should make an effort to explain what you believe. I respect any decision you make, as long as you really think about it carefully.

Love,

Anne

I took her advice and painstakingly wrote a letter to the school newspaper, explaining why I decided to go to the prom with a male date. The letter said that I hoped no one would be hurt by what I was doing, that a victory in court would be a victory for every Cumberland High student because it would be a blow against prejudice. The next issue of the school paper had space for all sorts of trivia, but my letter never appeared.

Later in April, the school theater group took its annual bus trip to New York City. Our teacher, Miss Frappier, was an exceptionally warm and friendly person and we were a tight-knit bunch—one of those rare groups of thespians whose members had no pent-up distrust or jealousy toward each other. On the bus Miss Frappier gave out the spring awards; I received one of them, for an outstanding performance in *A Thurber Carnival.*

In New York we went to the Guggenheim Museum and to a Broadway production of *They're Playing Our Song;* then when the group returned to Rhode Island, I stayed in New York to spend time with Paul.

Paul seemed to be getting happier in the city. Our friendship had not faded although Paul and I had not seen each other for months. We took a long walk through the Village, bringing each other up to date on what we'd been doing, and enjoying the feeling of the trees in bloom and spring in the air.

By evening I had settled any doubts I still had about who I wanted to invite to the prom. And so, with sweaty palms and butterflies in my stomach, I finally asked Paul: "I was wondering, um, do you have a date for the Cumberland High prom this year?"

Paul began laughing. "I'd love to attend the senior prom with you," he finally said. My feeling of happiness lasted all the way back to Rhode Island. [. . .]

When we arrived at the prom site, we were greeted with a glare of television lights. Flash bulbs were popping and everybody was talking and trying to ask questions as we walked toward the building. The reporters broke down the velvet ropes that were supposed to hold them back. I was too full of anticipation and excitement to think of anything to say. So a second before walking in the door, in a grand gesture of looniness, camp and high drama, I turned to the reporters, waved, and stuck out my tongue.

Once inside, Mr. Lynch quickly ushered Paul and me away from the door, so the reporters would be unable to see us. We were shown to an empty table, which neither of us enjoyed because there were no kids to talk to. My ninth-grade Spanish teacher, Mrs. Noelte, eventually sat with us.

Dinner was soon served. It was chicken cordon something or other, and consisted of mushed chicken encased in oil. My piece looked like a monster from the film *Alien.* The salad looked better, but when I bit into the cherry tomato, it splattered right onto my pants. I did my best to ignore the stain, but it kept showing up in the pictures people took.

After dinner was cleared away, many students began coming by to offer us a few good words. There was more good feeling than I would have anticipated. One after another, students came by and expressed their happiness that we could share the prom with each other. Billy Marlen came up and said he was glad to see us both. Even Dave Beamer approached and softly said, "I'm glad you're here."

Across the room, I noticed my old friend Bob Cote, accompanied by Bea Duvwalge. When Bob saw me he started to walk over, but Bea grabbed his arm and he went back to her.

I wandered over to a big picture window and stared out. Several reporters were talking outside on the lawn. For a moment I thought of all the people who would have enjoyed going to their proms with the date of their choice, but were denied that right; of all the people in the past who wanted to live respectably with the person they loved but could not; of all the men and women who had been hurt or killed because they were gay; and of the rich history of lesbians and homosexual men that had so long been ignored. Gradually we were triumphing over ignorance. One day we would be free.

The dance music came on. Kelleen Driskell came over and asked me to dance the first song with her. I was happy to accept. I'd known Kelleen in elementary school but I had drifted away from her, as from so many other people, during my fat years. We fast danced for that song and just through our physical movements together, without exchanging words, it felt as if we were reestablishing a communication.

After the dance I had to use the bathroom. Throughout the evening, Paul and I would see all kinds of defense mechanisms from the other guys whenever we went to the bathroom. Some of them made a beeline for the door as soon as we walked in. Others stayed, their desire to escape temporarily overcome by their curiosity about how gay people go to the bathroom.

When I got back to the dance floor, Paul asked me if I wanted to slow dance. I did. The next song was Bob Seger's "We've Got the Night," and we stepped out onto the dance floor.

The crowd receded. As I laid my head on Paul's shoulder, I saw a few students start to stare at us. I closed my eyes and listened to the music, my thoughts wandering over the events of that evening. When the song ended, I opened my eyes. A large crowd of students had formed a ring around us. Probably most of them had never before seen two happy men embracing in a slow dance. For a moment I was uncomfortable. Then I heard the sound that I knew so well as a B-52's fan. One of my favorite songs was coming up: "Rock Lobster."

Paul and I began dancing freestyle. Everyone else was still staring at us, but by the end of the first stanza, several couples had also begun dancing. The song has a contagious enthusiasm to it, and with each bar, more dancers came onto the dance floor.

I glanced over at the tables. Bob Cote was sitting with Bea Duvwalge, who was finishing off her chicken cordon-whatever. Bob was eyeing the dancing students and bouncing his leg with an obvious urge to join. He stood up and tugged at Bea's arm to come with him; she pulled him back and he sat down again with a look of disappointment.

More students were coming onto the floor to dance. I doubt that any two people were dancing with the same movements: the dancing was an expression of our individuality, and no one felt bad about being different. Everyone was free to be themselves.

A quarter of the way into the song, thirty people were on the dance floor. I looked at Bob and Bea again. Bea seemed to be wondering what a rock lobster was.

"Down, Down, Down," commanded the lyrics. Everyone on the dance floor sank to their knees and crouched on the ground. I lifted my head slightly to look around. Dozens of intertwining bodies crouched on their knees as if praying. We were all one; we shared a unity of pure love. And those who did not want to share it, such as Bea Duvwalge, sat on the sidelines. Bea was now arguing with Bob.

Red snappers snappin'
Clamshells clappin'

Everyone jumped to their feet again and resumed dancing. Many more kids had joined us and there must have been sixty or eighty people on the dance floor now.

As Paul and I danced, we had gradually drifted from our original space on the floor. We were now near the table where Bob and Bea sat. Out of the corner of my eye, I saw Bea suddenly stand up and grab a napkin. It looked like a glass of water had spilled on her. She dabbed at her gown.

"Down, Down, Down," cried the B-52's again, and we all went down. The feeling of unity among us permeated the air again. When we came up I heard Bea yelling at Bob, then she stormed off toward the bathroom. Now there were at least a hundred people on the dance floor. The tempo became more frenetic and everyone danced faster.

"Let's Rock!!!" bellowed from the speakers, and to my surprise, when I looked up I saw that Paul had disappeared. In his place was Bob Cote. I looked around; several other guys were dancing with each other, and girls were dancing with girls. Everybody was rockin', everybody was fruggin'. Who cared why? Maybe they were doing it to mock me and Paul, maybe they were doing it because they wanted to, maybe one was an excuse for the other. . . . I didn't know and I didn't care. It was fun. Everyone was together. Eventually Bob and I drifted away. I danced with girls, I danced with guys, I danced with the entire group.

Then the music stopped. "Rock Lobster" has an abrupt ending, and no one was quite ready for it to stop. I had been having so much fun that I lost track of time; I had also lost track of Paul, and had to look around for him.

I could see that everyone felt a sense of disorientation. For six minutes and forty-nine seconds, the students on the dance floor had forgotten about their defenses, forgotten about their shells. We just had fun.

Large Group Exercise: Common Ground on Gender

Approximate time: one to two class sessions

What concerns do the participants have and want to share about issues of gender? Common Ground is designed to encourage the sharing of thoughts and feelings about a particular issue. As with other exercises in *Dealing With Differences,* Common Ground depends on participants being respectful of each other and assuming responsibility for the process.

SUPPLIES: Chalkboard and chalk or poster paper and marking pens.

STUDENT LEADERSHIP: Two or more students volunteer to begin the sharing of concerns and to record a summary of the concerns and the results of the large group discussion on the chalkboard or poster paper.

TO BEGIN: The participants form a circle. One person volunteers to be the first to share a concern he or she has about the topic under discussion. This person moves inside the circle and speaks the concern.

Here are some examples of concerns about gender taken from our pilot program Dealing With Prejudice:

I'm concerned because our shop teacher thinks that girls can't do anything, and says things like, "I don't want to be around when you ladies learn to drive."

I'm concerned because my brother felt he had to transfer to a different high school, because he likes art and drama and that didn't fit the macho image of boys at his old school.

I'm concerned because I've dated a lot of different guys, and people—even people I thought were my friends—are calling me horrible names.

I'm concerned because my mother's a lesbian, and it hurts me when I hear people making fun of lesbians in the cafeteria or in homeroom.

Participants who feel that they share the concern expressed—who identify with the speaker because similar things have happened to them or to people they care about—join the speaker inside the circle. These participants can exchange greetings and speak about their identification with the concern if they wish.

After a few minutes, all of these participants move back to the larger circle and another person moves inside the circle with a concern. This person is joined by the individuals who share his or her concern. After a few minutes of conversation, these participants move back.

The process of sharing concerns continues until everyone has had the opportunity to speak, although not everyone may decide to speak.

The participants return to their seats. They take five to ten minutes to summarize the concerns raised in the exercise. An exercise leader writes this summary on the chalkboard or poster paper.

QUESTIONS FOR REFLECTION AND LARGE GROUP DISCUSSION

- Which concerns do I identify or agree with?
- Which concerns do I not identify or agree with?
- How did I feel about the way other participants were responding to my concerns?
- What surprised me about this exercise?

Small Group Exercise: Gender—Concerns and Suggestions for Action

Approximate time: two class sessions

What concerns about gender are most important to the participants? What actions can they take to address these concerns? To explore these questions, participants assemble in the small groups formed in Chapter 2.

Action can take a variety of forms, both individual and collective. It is important that the actions students suggest—however small or incremental—are taken seriously by teachers and administrators and encouraged whenever possible. If teachers dismiss or discourage suggestions for action, students may justly complain that the program is hypocritical or irrelevant to their lives. Here are some examples of actions suggested and taken by students in the pilot program Dealing With Prejudice:

1. Speak up more for yourself and for others in the face of prejudice

2. Form an after-school discussion/action group

3. Go as a class or group to a relevant movie and discuss it afterward

4. Watch as a class or group relevant videos or TV programs

5. Read books and magazines about your concern

6. Write or call the local newspaper, radio station, or TV station about your concern

7. Boycott businesses that ignore or contribute to your concern

8. Meet as a group with school administrators about you concern

9. Volunteer with an existing school, church, or community group that works on your concern

10. Hold a student-run school assembly on your concern

11. Develop a play or presentation on your concern and perform it for the entire school

12. Develop a display or exhibit on your concern in the classroom or elsewhere on school property

SUPPLIES: Poster paper and marking pens.

STUDENT LEADERSHIP: One student in each small group volunteers to record the results of the group's discussion on poster paper.

TO BEGIN: Each small group chooses one concern to explore from the list developed and recorded during Common Ground. The group recorder then writes these four column heads on poster paper:

What do we know (about this concern)?

What do we need to know (about this concern)?

How can we know (about this concern)?

How can we act (on this concern)?

Using as a guideline the principles of critical thinking and I-search described in Chapter 2, each group brainstorms the concern it has chosen. Groups may consult with teachers on completing this process through trips to the school or the public library, or calls to or meetings with community members. Teachers and students decide together how much I-search can be done during the *Dealing With Differences* sessions and how much can be done outside of class.

When I-search is completed, each small group's recorder summarizes the group's findings on a sheet of poster paper and posts it on the wall to be read and considered by the other participants.

Large Group Exercise: Gender— Concerns and Suggestions for Action

Approximate time: two class sessions

In this exercise, participants reflect on the results of the small group discussions and decide which suggestions for action they can implement as individuals, as small groups, or as a class.

SUPPLIES: Chalkboard and chalk or poster paper and marking pens.

STUDENT LEADERSHIP: Two or more students volunteer to give instructions for the exercise and to record the results of the large group discussion on the chalkboard or poster paper.

TO BEGIN: The exercise leaders ask the participants to leave their desks to read the posted results of each small group's discussion. Participants are encouraged to ask questions of one another and to make notes on what they find interesting.

After 10 to 20 minutes of mingling, all participants return to their seats for discussion.

QUESTIONS FOR REFLECTION AND LARGE GROUP DISCUSSION

- Now that I have reviewed all of the suggestions for action, what suggestions would I most like to implement?

- Are these actions I can take as an individual? As part of a group? As a member of this class?

- What help do I need from other participants (students or teachers) to take action?

- What help do I need from people outside the classroom (administrators, community members, family) to take action?

Guest Speaker on Gender

Approximate time: one to two class sessions

At this point, after the participants have discussed gender, sexism, heterosexism, their concerns, and their suggestions for action, we recommend that they invite a guest into the classroom to engage in a dialogue with the participants on issues of gender. We recommend that the speaker be someone who not only works on issues of gender but also has lived experience with these issues. It would be significant if the speaker were a friend or family member of one of the participants.

Local social service organizations, university or college departments of women's and gay studies, and advocacy organizations such as the American Association of University Women (AAUW), National Organization for Women (NOW), and Parents and Friends of Lesbians and Gays (PFLAG) may be able to provide or recommend speakers.

Gender and Self-Esteem in School

Approximate time: two class sessions

Self-esteem means to have a good opinion of oneself and one's abilities—who you are and what you think you can do. In relationship to schooling, self-esteem falls into two categories: *academic self-esteem,* having a good opinion of yourself and performance in the classroom, and *personal self-esteem,* having a good opinion of yourself and your abilities outside the classroom (AAUW, 1991).

The two types of self-esteem are related but not the same. Some students make high grades and please their teachers but have dangerously low personal self-esteem because they have poor self-images and poor relationships with family and friends. Others make low grades and are not favored by their teachers but have high personal self-esteem because they have good self-images and feel that they excel in areas outside the classroom—in sports, in work, in caring for their families and friends (Orenstein, 1994).

Adolescence—the junior high and high school years—is a time in which self-esteem drops, for both boys and girls. Girls, however, experience sharper drops in self-esteem than do boys. In one study, researchers showed that in elementary school 69% of boys and 60% of girls said that they were "happy the way I am." In high school, however, only 46% of boys and 29% of girls said that they were "happy the way I am" (AAUW, 1991).

The self-esteem of white girls and of Hispanic girls drops sharply by adolescence. The only girls who as a group maintain relatively high self-esteem from elementary school to high school are African Americans. In elementary school, 65% say that they "are happy the way I am," a figure that drops only 7 points, to 58%, in high school (AAUW, 1991).

African American girls may as a group have much higher personal self-esteem than academic self-esteem. The Simmons College professor Janie Victoria Ward, who has done research on African-

American girls, states, "Black girls seem to be maintaining high levels of self-esteem by disassociating themselves from school. . . . There is high self-esteem among black girls because black culture emphasizes independence and assertiveness. But academic self-esteem is low" (AAUW, 1991, p. 27).

Boys, too, experience moments of resistance to unfairness, which often go unrecognized by other people. This occurs particularly for boys who may not fit the gender construct of masculinity as defined by teachers, parents, and peers. In adolescence, however, many boys remain more confident and more focused on their talents and goals than girls do. When asked what they like about themselves, girls are twice as likely as boys to mention not a talent but something about their appearance—their hair, their eyes, their clothes (AAUW, 1991).

QUESTIONS FOR REFLECTION AND LARGE GROUP DISCUSSION

- What and who has influenced my self-esteem, particularly as I have become a teenager?

- Is there a difference between my academic self-esteem and my personal self-esteem?

- How has gender influenced my self-esteem? How has race influenced my self-esteem? How has class influenced my self-esteem?

Individual Exercise: Reading and Reflection— "One Sister's Love of Beauty"

Approximate time: two class sessions

Before the next class session, the participants read "One Sister's Love of Beauty" by Vanessa May. This essay may be read aloud in class (or signed, using American Sign Language) if participants feel that doing so would deepen their responses to it.

The participants prepare reflections on the poem in a form that displays one or more of their multiple intelligences (see Chapter 2)—an essay, a poem, a rap, a song, a dance, a drawing, an equation, a journal entry, a video, or an image. These reflections may be used in group exhibits or displays, in presentations or assemblies, or in individual portfolios.

In preparing their reflections, participants keep in mind the following questions:

QUESTIONS FOR READING AND REFLECTION

- What emotions did this reading evoke in me?

- What lived experience (mine or someone else's) did this reading make me remember?

- What did the reading tell me that I already know and think is important?

- What did the reading tell me that I didn't know and want to know more about?

In the next class sessions, the participants volunteer to share their reflections. Every participant should have a chance to share his or her reflection, although not every participant may choose to do so.

One Sister's Love of Beauty*

Vanessa May

Vanessa May, who lives in Los Angeles, California, is an aspiring lawyer as well as a poet and essayist. She wrote "One Sister's Love of Beauty" to affirm women of color and all those who do not fit conventional standards of beauty.

Beautiful smiles on beautiful faces, each one's roots from different places, but all finding asylum on the lunch benches of Brainard Avenue's elementary school.

Beautiful, wondrous world sisters whose cultures spanned the globe. Latin America, Europe, Asia, and Africa. Susan Rico. Mindy Nakamura. Barbara Rivers. Tracy Sketerman. Lisa Belson.** Vanessa May*

Sisters of Gaea, daughters of Eve, all finding a common ground on which to stand and to communicate. Enjoying each other's company and appreciating our differences.

That is, until fifth grade, when the joys of childhood became the pangs of prepubescence. One's racial, cultural, sexual, and social identities were questioned. Are you Black? Are you trying to be white? Are you fruity? Are you cool? Are you? What are you?

It was during this time that societal constructs laid siege to free hearts, minds, and souls. White girls do not hang out with Black girls unless they want to be Black. Asian girls don't hang

**AUTHOR'S NOTE: These names are pseudonyms.

out with Mexicans unless they wanna be Mexican. Girls must like boys unless they are weird, and you must have certain clothes to define you and the group to which you belong. Conform or rebel. Something that all preteens and teens do, to a greater or lesser degree.

Our society sets into motion divide-and-conquer tactics that rip at the very essence of our being. To question societal constructs is to live a life of one's own making, and how many of us can create for ourselves a mode of behavior that will allow for existence in a society that by design systematically destroys deviance?

Moreover, people are taught that in order to be truly socialized one must act in a manner that doesn't deviate far from Puritanical European roots. Prosperous roots that built one of the mightiest nations the world has ever known. A nation whose reputation is based on exported lies and untruths. A nation that holds all other nations captive. Nations, striving to be like her, engage in a process that is destroying the world.

How?

First: indoctrinate people with the inane idea that white is powerful. It appears to be so. Modern history shows us white world domination. The subjugation of people of color worldwide gives an appearance of power—not the reality of a paranoid humanoid whose fear of extinction causes it to destroy all that seems to threaten it.

Second: indoctrinate people with the insane idea that the way in which they have lived for thousands of years is wrong, "primitive." Compare a grass hut to a skyscraper. Compare hunting and gathering food every day with going to the refrigerator or McDonald's. Don't discuss the reality of ecologically unsound structures that recycle stale air, spread disease, and create waste in such amounts that we can't dispose of it. Ignore the reality that hunting and gathering places in perspective—the value of life and death, need and want, animals, plants, and humans and our interdependence.

In conclusion: create a zero-sum social construct that teaches superiority based on innate inferiority and teach *all* people to aspire to it. In their aspiration they continually lose but appear to gain. The model appears to continually gain power, wealth, position, and value; all the while it wreaks havoc in order to keep up appearances. In reality we all lose.

Societal constructs lay siege to young, impressionable minds, hearts, and souls. Taught not to appreciate our distinct and unique cultures, we are taught instead to treat them with mistrust and suspicion. Sell out. Renounce your family's ways, adopt a prepackaged social identity. You must fit into one of them but it cannot, it *must* not, be based on your own culture or on an eclectic multicultural view. It must be based on white supremacy, based of the idea that you and other people of color are inferior. Not just your looks, but your actions. You cannot be civil toward each other because in your quest to be like white, you must all fight for its favor.

Can we cease to care about how we are seen in the eyes of our lighter kin? Can we see ourselves with our own eyes? Can we find the beauty in ourselves? Can we see with wisdom, the eternal wisdom each young child has that assures that we all are one? A wisdom that lets the soul see, the heart act, and the mind think.

I love beauty. Beauty to me comes in all shades, shapes, and sizes. I must see life this way. I can also see ugliness. It too comes in all shades, shapes, and sizes. What differentiates beauty from what is ugly is behavior. Western society directs people to see beauty with only one vision. (Note the *Miss Universe Pageant:* The majority of the world's people are people of color, yet the majority of the contestants of the pageant are white-skinned.)

I let my mind open and the ideas come forth. I cannot help my love of beauty. I cannot quell my love of life. I cannot be blinded, nor let others define my visions. I know what I see.

Sisterfriends, you all are very beautiful! Now, I know I've never seen you, but Beauty can be felt as well as seen; and I feel your beauty.

My definition of beauty is not based on any European standard or any European mind-set. If it were, I would hate myself, and probably hate or envy you. I've come to understand that beauty truly is in the eye and soul of the beholder. Understanding this has made me an extremely happy woman. I take sheer delight in appreciating my fellow human beings and in appreciating all that this world and life has to offer.

Women of color, particularly African American women, have been debased and devalued based on their hue. For "some strange reason," the lighter hued and more European the woman looks, the more beautiful she is viewed as being. In essence, beauty standards are deeply rooted in racism and colorism.

I know I'm not telling you anything you weren't aware of when you woke up this morning. Right? The thing is, how many of you buy this Western European standard? I mean, don't believe the hype, don't subscribe to the stereotype. 'Cuz every time you do, you are helping to perpetuate the myth of white supremacy, and this argues against the genetic annihilation of whites. Strong words, huh? Well, as Malcolm X said, "Too black, too strong."

Personal experience has taught me to hold my darker-hued sister in great regard. She has endured a lot. I've heard brothers and sisters talk about a person being too dark, having too big a nose, too-nappy hair, or too-large lips. Every time I hear this, I cringe. It is obvious to me that such utterances are outright condemnations of all African physical traits, particular sub-Saharan African traits. Traits that most African-Americans can trace in their ancestry. Come on, how can the physical characteristics of the original people be ugly!

Unfortunately, from the cradle to the grave, we are bombarded with the lie that "white is right." This mind-set originated in Europe and has been barbarously spread across the globe. It started during the age of exploration and did the most damage during the years of slavery, imperialism, and colonialism. These actions led to the physical and mental subjugation of people of color worldwide. This subjugation was not based and is not based on one group's superiority or inferiority, but on one group's quest for self-preservation. It is a defense mechanism used to ensure the perpetuation of genetically recessive traits.

The real trip is that the biggest threat to this world order is the African. This is why Africans are the most oppressed people. Basically, the darker and more physically African, the greater the threat. Just think, if the world's people were to come together in peace and love, then what would we be made of? What would we look like?

You dig?

It seems to me that the young African Americans of today define "blackness" in a very superficial way: by one's clothes, one's musical tastes, and of course, by one's skin color. But this all must go if we as a people are to ever love and respect ourselves. I have seen the sorrow in the face of a beautiful ebony woman who realizes that the reason her butterscotch friend is getting hawked by the men is because she's light. I have seen the anguish in the mixed kid who, try as she might, can never succeed at being black enough to be black or white enough to be white. I have seen the names "tar baby," "liver lips," "nap head," "high yellow nigga" . . . elicit rivers of tears. Honestly, I have seen enough.

6

Disability and Ableism

*Disability culture. **Say what?** Aren't
disabled people just isolated victims of
nature or circumstance?*

*Yes and no. True, we are far too often
isolated. Locked away in the pits, closets
and institutions of enlightened societies
everywhere. But there is a growing
consciousness among us: "that is not
acceptable." Because there is always an
underground. Notes get passed among
survivors. And the notes we're passing
these days say, "there's power in difference.
Power. Pass the word."*

—Cheryl Marie Wade (1994, p. 15)

Disability *(dis + ability) has been defined since the 17th century
as a physical or mental condition—usually permanent—that limits
an individual's activities, especially the ability to work (New
Shorter Oxford English Dictionary, 1993). Since the 1970s, however, some persons with disabilities have developed a new definition
of the word, one that has focused on two issues. The first is a quest
for opportunity and inclusion in society—including opportunities
for employment, education, communication, and access to public*

buildings and transportation. The second is a search for a disability culture, a sense of being different that is positive, proud, and powerful (Longmore, 1995).

In this chapter, the participants explore their own ideas and feelings about disability and difference, the construction of disability, ableism and its relationships to other prejudices, the experiences of persons with disabilities, and suggestions for action on disability issues in the classroom and the community.

This chapter contains the following sections. The times given to complete them are approximate.

Icebreaker: "Labels" (one to two class sessions)
What Is Disability? (two class sessions)
Large Group Exercise: DISABILITY and VALUE (one class session)
Ableism (two to three class sessions)
Individual Exercise: Media Images of Disability (one to two class sessions)
Large Group Exercise: Common Ground on Disability (one to two class sessions)
Small Group Exercise: Disability—Concerns and Suggestions for Action (two class sessions)
Large Group Exercise: Disability—Concerns and Suggestions for Action (two class sessions)
Guest Speaker on Disability (one to two class sessions)
Individual Exercise: Reading and Reflection—"Lunch Break" (two class sessions)
Institutional and Cultural Ableism in the Classroom (two class sessions)
Individual Exercise: Reading and Reflection—"Giving It Back" (two class sessions)

Icebreaker: "Labels"

Approximate time: one to two class sessions

Are individuals labeled according to what their bodies and minds can and cannot do? Does the assignment of a label influence the ways in which an individual is treated? Do labels make individuals more aware of their differences, or of their similarities?

In the exercise "Labels," participants examine how both wearing a label and being aware of the labels given to others influences thoughts, words, and actions. As with other exercises in *Dealing With Differences,* "Labels" depends on the participants being respectful of each other and assuming responsibility for the process.

SUPPLIES: Chalkboard and chalk or poster paper and marking pens, construction paper and tape.

STUDENT LEADERSHIP: Two or more students volunteer to help to prepare and hand out labels, give instructions, and record the results of the large group discussion on the chalkboard or poster paper.

PREPARATION (done before class): The exercise leaders cut light-colored construction paper into pieces large enough to be seen throughout the classroom. They then write one of the following labels on each piece of paper. The labels should be repeated to ensure that there is one label for every participant. At least one label (for example, "PERSON WHO IS BLIND") should be repeated three times so that the participants wearing that label constitute a group. After the labels are complete, the exercise leaders shuffle them and place them face down on a desk or table.

LABELS:
PERSON WHO IS BLIND
PERSON WHO IS DEAF
PERSON WHO USES A WHEELCHAIR
PERSON WITH SEVERE SCARS
PERSON WITH EPILEPSY
PERSON WITH DIABETES
PERSON WITH DOWN SYNDROME
PERSON WITH MULTIPLE SCLEROSIS
PERSON WITH RHEUMATOID ARTHRITIS
PERSON WITH CEREBRAL PALSY
PERSON WITH ALZHEIMER'S DISEASE
PERSON WITH SCHIZOPHRENIA
PERSON WITH DEPRESSION
PERSON WITH AMPUTATED LEG
PERSON WITH AIDS
PERSON WITH PARALYZED ARM
PERSON WHO WEIGHS FOUR HUNDRED POUNDS
PERSON WHO STUTTERS

TO BEGIN: The exercise leaders ask the participants to move their desks into a large circle or semicircle so that there is an open space in the middle of the classroom. The exercise leaders then ask the participants to come up to the front of the classroom one by one to receive a label. Each participant's label is taped to his or her back so that he or she cannot see it. (No participant should directly tell another participant what is on his or her label.) The exercise leaders complete the labeling process by taping labels onto each other's backs.

Participants mingle in the open space, saying hello to and making conversation with as many other participants as they can. These conversations may provide clues to the labels that have been assigned. Mingling can continue for 10 to 20 minutes, depending on the depth of the conversations among participants.

After 10 to 20 minutes, the exercise leaders ask the participants to remove and read their labels, allowing a few moments for reaction. Then the participants return to their seats for discussion.

QUESTIONS FOR REFLECTION AND LARGE GROUP DISCUSSION

- Which label did I have the hardest time responding to?
- Which label did I have the easiest time responding to?
- How did I feel about the way other participants were responding to me?
- How did I feel when I learned what was on my label?
- What surprised me about this exercise?

What Is Disability?

Approximate time: two class sessions

"There are hundreds of different disabilities," Joseph Shapiro (1993) points out in *No Pity: People With Disabilities Forging a New Civil Rights Movement.*

> Some are congenital [occurring at birth]; most come later in life. Some are progressive [becoming more serious over time], like muscular dystrophy, cystic fibrosis, and some forms of vision and hearing loss. Others, like seizure conditions, are episodic [occurring from time to time]. Multiple sclerosis is episodic and progressive. Some conditions are static, like the loss of a limb. Still others, like cancer and occasionally paralysis, can even go away. Some disabilities are "hidden," like epilepsy or diabetes. Disability law also applies to people with perceived disabilities such as obesity or stuttering, which are not disabling but create prejudice and discrimination. Each disability comes in differing degrees of severity. (p. 5)

In 1991, by some federal estimates the number of persons in the United States with disabilities was 43 million—one in six Americans. This figure did not include individuals with AIDS and HIV, learning disabilities, and some mental and physical disabilities. Even at 43 million, persons with disabilities could be considered the largest minority group in the United States (Shapiro, 1993).

Many persons who have disabilities do not want to be identified as disabled. Their reluctance stems more from the social effects of disability than from its physical and mental effects. Viewed in this way, disability—like class, race, and gender (see Chapters 3, 4, and 5) is a *construct,* a social concept or idea. Individuals, communities, and institutions develop constructs about disability—as about race, gender, and class—to make sense of the world in which they live and to gain control of the world in which they live. The key to the construction of disability is not the physical or mental differences that exist among different people, but the ways in which value is assigned to these differences (Rothenberg, 1992). Acknowledging difference is merely saying that X is different from Y; assigning value to difference is saying that X is superior or inferior to Y.

Traditional constructs of disability are that to be disabled is to be cursed, sinful, or pitiful. There are examples of these constructs in the Bible, in classical literature, and in modern horror movies. Job in the Old Testament sees his skin disease as a sign of disfavor from God. William Shakespeare invented a hunchback for his King Richard III—the historical Richard did not have one—to make the character seem more evil. Tiny Tim, the child who uses crutches in Charles Dickens's *A Christmas Carol,* is sweet and brave but also helpless and possibly doomed. Danny DeVito's Penguin in the movie *Batman Returns,* abandoned as a baby in the sewers of Gotham City because he has flippers instead of hands, is like Tiny Tim grown up to be a bitter monster (Shapiro, 1993).

Another construct of disability—one that has developed in the 20th century—is the "medical model" (Longmore, 1995, p. 5). In this view, disability is an illness to be cured or a defect to be corrected. Under the medical model, persons with disabilities must undergo treatment in hospitals and other institutions. If their conditions are corrected or cured, they are welcomed back into society; if not, they must remain outside society, often in institutions.

Some persons with disabilities oppose events such as the Jerry Lewis Labor Day telethon for the Muscular Dystrophy Association. Although these individuals recognize the need to raise money for services and research, they see telethons as reinforcing unfair and limiting constructs. One is the old pity construct—persons with disabilities are helpless, childlike Tiny Tims. The other is the newer medical construct—persons with disabilities must wait for cures in order to lead full and independent lives (Shapiro, 1993).

It is only since the 1970s that some individuals with disabilities have started to use *disability, disabled,* and *person with a disability* as new constructs, terms that acknowledge an individual's condition and particular needs without implying that she or he is cursed, sinful, to be pitied, or to be cured. The difference between saying "Julia is a person with mental retardation" and "Julia is retarded" is that the first statement puts Julia the person first, whereas the second implies that Julia's disability is all there is to her. The difference between saying "Jim uses a wheelchair" and "Jim is wheelchair-bound" is that the first statement makes it clear that Jim needs a wheelchair to get around, whereas the second implies that Jim is trapped and helpless.

Some persons with disabilities have gone even farther, reclaiming among themselves the Old English word *cripple* as a sign of defiance and pride rather than of fear and shame. "It's like a raised gnarled fist," says Cheryl Marie Wade (Shapiro, 1993, p. 34). Wade, a California artist, is one of the founders of a performance group called the Wry Crips, which writes and acts in pieces based on its members' life experiences.

A slang term used by some persons with disabilities for persons without disabilities is TABs, for temporarily able-bodied people. This is a reminder that any individual can become disabled at any time and that 85% of persons with disabilities acquired their disabilities not at birth but sometime later in life (Shapiro, 1993). Disability is an experience that can divide and isolate, but it is also an experience that can unite. According to Patrisha Wright, who when interviewed by Joseph Shapiro (1993) worked as a national disabilities activist in Washington, D.C., "It doesn't matter if your name is Kennedy or Rockefeller, or Smith or Jones, your family's been touched" (p. 8).

QUESTIONS FOR REFLECTION AND LARGE GROUP DISCUSSION

- What is my lived experience with disability?
- Who and what have influenced my thoughts and feelings about disability?
- What constructs of disability have I used to make sense of my world? To gain control over my world?

Large Group Exercise: DISABILITY and VALUE

Approximate time: one class session

In this exercise, the participants examine their ideas about the differences of persons with disabilities and the values assigned to those differences through both traditional and new constructs of disability.

SUPPLIES: Chalkboard and chalk or poster paper and marking pens.
STUDENT LEADERSHIP: One student volunteers to be the recorder for this exercise.
TO BEGIN: The recorder writes the words DISABILITY and VALUE at the heads of two columns on the chalkboard or poster paper.

Participants suggest words or phrases that they feel express the differences of persons with disabilities. The recorder writes these phrases in the DISABILITY column. Participants suggest words or phrases that express values assigned to those differences. The recorder writes these phrases in the VALUE column. (To give one example: DEAF could be assigned both the value CAN'T COMMUNICATE WITH OTHER PEOPLE and the value HAS OWN LANGUAGE AND COMMUNITY.)

QUESTIONS FOR REFLECTION AND LARGE GROUP DISCUSSION

- What values do I associate with disabilities?
- Which of these values has been influenced by traditional constructs of disability?
- Which of these values has been influenced by newer constructs of disability?
- What surprised me about this exercise?

Ableism

Approximate time: two to three class sessions

Ableism, a term dating from the late 20th century, refers both to the belief that persons with disabilities are inferior to persons without disabilities and to practices of discrimination and violence against persons with disabilities. The three categories of racism defined in Chapter 4 (Barndt, 1991) can also be applied to ableism: *individual ableism,* the prejudices held by a particular person; *cultural ableism,* the prejudices held by members of a particular culture or community; and *institutional ableism,* a system of economic and social discrimination against persons with disabilities. Institutional ableism can be defined as "prejudice plus power" (Barndt, 1991, p. 28).

In individual ableism, both persons with disabilities and persons without disabilities believe and act on traditional constructs of disability (disability as curse, disability as sin or evil, disability as something to be pitied, disability as something to be corrected or cured). "I used to know what I would wish for," a young woman who used crutches said during a demonstration of persons with disabilities in 1977. "I wanted to be beautiful. I wanted to stop being a cripple. But now I know I am beautiful" (Shapiro, 1993, p. 69).

Some acts of individual ableism are deliberate. Kathi Wolfe (1994) had such an experience in Washington, D.C., in April 1993. As she approached tables of people distributing pamphlets and buttons for a gay and lesbian rights march, Wolfe was assaulted by a young man described as a skinhead who threw her white cane to the ground, saying, "Get out of the way, blind lady! You and these queers belong in concentration camps" (p. 213).

Some acts of individual ableism are unconscious. Marylou Breslin, at the time the director of the California-based Disability Rights and Education Fund, was waiting at an airport for a plane, dressed in a suit and carrying a briefcase, when another business-woman walked by and flipped a quarter into the coffee cup Breslin was holding, spilling coffee all over Breslin's blouse. Because Breslin uses a battery-powered wheelchair, the other woman had assumed that she was begging for spare change. Realizing her mistake, the embarrassed passerby hurried away (Shapiro, 1993).

Cultural ableism—deeply held social attitudes about disability—can be found, as mentioned, in sources as diverse as the Bible, Shakespeare, and Batman movies. Like individual ableism, cultural ableism is sometimes unconscious. As mentioned earlier, some individuals with disabilities consider the Jerry Lewis telethon to be an instance of cultural ableism because it portrays persons with disabilities as childlike, dependent, and waiting for cures, although it raises money for and awareness of persons with disabilities.

Institutional ableism is an inherent bias against persons with disability built into the structures of society. A person with a wheelchair not being able to work because her city does not have wheelchair-accessible buses is an example of institutional ableism. A person with a disability deciding not to take a job because if he does he will lose government benefits that pay for the personal care attendant he needs to help him bathe and dress is another example of institutional ableism.

The word *institutional* has a particular meaning for persons with disabilities. One of the most striking examples of institutional ableism is that many persons with disabilities, deprived of other choices, have lived and still live in institutions such as state hospitals and nursing homes.

In the first half of the 20th century, this practice was defended as being for the good of society, "prevent[ing] those who are manifestly unfit from continuing their kind," the Supreme Court Justice Oliver Wendell Holmes wrote in 1927 (quoted in Shapiro, 1993, p. 158). Since World War II, this practice has been defended as being good for persons with disabilities, despite the fact that those who are institutionalized often get little activity or attention.

Since the early 1980s, new social programs have given some persons with disabilities the opportunity to move out of institutions and into group homes or their own apartments and to hold jobs. Jeff Gunderson is one such person. Gunderson, born with cerebral palsy and using a wheelchair, lived in two Wisconsin nursing homes with mostly elderly people from the time he was 18 until he was 27. His mother could no longer provide the personal services he needed and his Medicaid coverage would pay for a nursing home but not a personal attendant. While in the nursing home, Gunderson was forced to watch soap operas all day, eat bland gruel, and go to bed at 7 p.m. When Gunderson rebelled at these restrictions, attendants punished him by tying him to his bed or dragging him into cold showers. Gunderson feared that he would never leave the nursing home (Shapiro, 1993).

After moving to an apartment with a personal care attendant in 1981, Gunderson was able to shop, work, talk on the phone, watch movies and football with friends, and bowl. "I can go out and do things for myself now," he said. "I used to be a shy person because of all those years living in a nursing home" (quoted in Shapiro, 1993, p. 240).

QUESTIONS FOR REFLECTION AND LARGE GROUP DISCUSSION

- Have I witnessed or experienced ableism? When and how?

- Are these experiences examples of individual ableism? Cultural ableism? Institutional ableism?

- What relationships do I see between ableism and other prejudices?

Individual Exercise: Media Images of Disability

Approximate time: one to two class sessions

What cultural images of disability exist in the mass media—newspapers, magazines, books, movies, television, music? Do these images portray traditional constructs of disability? Newer constructs of disability? Both traditional and newer constructs of disability?

In this exercise, participants can choose to do one, two, or all three of the following out-of-class assignments to explore the ways in which disability is portrayed in our society.

OPTION A: Select one image (photograph, advertisement, illustration, political cartoon) that expresses something you find significant about persons with disabilities or the constructs of disability discussed in this chapter. Prepare a brief oral or written reflection on the image to share in class.

OPTION B: Watch television over the course of a week and note how disability and persons with disabilities are portrayed in commercials, drama shows, comedy shows, and documentaries or news broadcasts. Prepare a brief oral or written report to share in class.

OPTION C: Review a fairy tale or other children's story and note how it portrays disability and persons with disabilities. Prepare a brief oral or written report to share in class.

In the next class or classes, each participant needs to have the opportunity to share his or her report, although not everyone may choose to speak. After the sharing of reports is completed, the participants may choose to make a collage or display of their images and reports in the classroom or in another area of the school.

QUESTIONS FOR REFLECTION AND LARGE GROUP DISCUSSION

- What constructs of disability are displayed by the medium I chose to report on (image, television programs, fairy tale, or children's story)?
- How are the constructs I discovered similar to the constructs discovered by other participants?
- How are the constructs I discovered different from those discovered by other participants?
- What surprised me about this exercise?

Large Group Exercise: Common Ground on Disability

Approximate time: one to two class sessions

What concerns do the participants have and want to share about issues of disability? Common Ground is designed to encourage the sharing of thoughts and feelings about a particular issue. As with other exercises in *Dealing With Differences,* Common Ground depends on participants being respectful of each other and assuming responsibility for the process.

SUPPLIES: Chalkboard and chalk or poster paper and marking pens.

STUDENT LEADERSHIP: Two or more students volunteer to begin the sharing of concerns and to record a summary of the concerns and the results of the large group discussion on the chalkboard or poster paper.

TO BEGIN: The participants form a circle. One person then volunteers to be the first to share a concern he or she has about the topic under discussion. This person moves inside the circle and speaks the concern.

Here are some examples of concerns about disability:

I'm concerned because our school didn't have wheelchair ramps or lifts, and when I became disabled, I had to fight to keep going here.

I'm concerned because people treat me like I'm stupid because I'm in the lowest track classes of the school.

I'm concerned because my grandma has been diagnosed with Alzheimer's disease and some of my relatives are treating her like she's not really a person any more.

I'm concerned because people make fun of the birthmark on my face all the time.

Participants who feel that they share the concern expressed—who identify with the speaker because similar things have happened to them or to people they care about—join the speaker inside the circle. These participants can exchange greetings and speak about their identification with the concern if they wish.

After a few minutes, all of these participants move back to the larger circle and another person moves inside the circle with a concern. This person is joined by the individuals who share his or her concern. After a few minutes of conversation, these participants move back.

The process of sharing concerns continues until everyone has had the opportunity to speak, although not everyone may decide to speak.

The participants return to their seats. They take five to ten minutes to summarize the concerns raised in the exercise. An exercise leader writes this summary on the chalkboard or poster paper.

QUESTIONS FOR REFLECTION AND LARGE GROUP DISCUSSION

- Which concerns do I identify or agree with?

- Which concerns do I not identify or agree with?

- How did I feel about the way other participants were responding to my concerns?

- What surprised me about this exercise?

Small Group Exercise: Disability— Concerns and Suggestions for Action

Approximate time: two class sessions

What concerns about disability are most important to the participants? What actions can they take to address these concerns? To explore these questions, the participants assemble in the small groups formed in Chapter 2.

Action can take a variety of forms, both individual and collective. It is important that the actions students suggest—however small or incremental—are taken seriously by teachers and administrators and encouraged whenever possible. If teachers dismiss or discourage suggestions for action, students may justly complain that the program is hypocritical or irrelevant to their lives. Some examples of actions suggested and taken by students in the pilot program Dealing With Prejudice:

1. Speak up more for yourself and for others in the face of prejudice

2. Form an after-school discussion/action group

3. Go as a class or group to a relevant movie and discuss it afterward

4. Watch as a class or group relevant videos or TV programs

5. Read books and magazines about your concern

6. Write or call the local newspaper, radio station, or TV station about your concern

7. Boycott businesses that ignore or contribute to your concern

8. Meet as a group with school administrators about your concern

9. Volunteer with an existing school, church, or community group that works on your concern

10. Hold a student-run school assembly on your concern

11. Develop a play or presentation on your concern and perform it for the entire school

12. Develop a display or exhibit on your concern in the classroom or elsewhere on school property

SUPPLIES: Poster paper and marking pens.

STUDENT LEADERSHIP: One student in each small group volunteers to record the results of the group's discussion on poster paper.

TO BEGIN: Each small group chooses one concern to explore from the list developed and recorded during Common Ground. The group recorder then writes these four column heads on a sheet of poster paper:

What do we know (about this concern)?

What do we need to know (about this concern)?

How can we know (about this concern)?

How can we act (on this concern)?

Using as a guideline the principles of critical thinking and I-search described in Chapter 2, each group brainstorms the concern it has chosen. Groups may consult with teachers on completing this process through trips to the school or the public library, or calls to or meetings with community members. Teachers and students decide together how much I-search can be done during the *Dealing With Differences* sessions and how much can be done outside of class.

When I-search is completed, each small group's recorder summarizes the group's findings on a sheet of poster paper and posts it on the wall to be read and considered by other participants.

Large Group Exercise: Disability— Concerns and Suggestions for Action

Approximate time: two class sessions

In this exercise, the participants reflect on the results of the small group discussions and decide which suggestions for action they can implement as individuals, as small groups, or as a class.

SUPPLIES: Chalkboard and chalk or poster paper and marking pens.

STUDENT LEADERSHIP: Two or more students volunteer to give instructions for the exercise and to record the results of the large group discussion on the chalkboard or poster paper.

TO BEGIN: The exercise leaders ask the participants to leave their desks to read the posted results of each small group's discussion. Participants are encouraged to ask questions of one another and to make notes on what they find interesting.

After 10 to 20 minutes of mingling, the participants return to their seats for discussion.

QUESTIONS FOR REFLECTION AND LARGE GROUP DISCUSSION

- Now that I have reviewed all of the suggestions for action, what suggestions would I most like to implement?

- Are these actions I can take as an individual? As part of a group? As a member of this class?

- What help do I need from other participants (students or teachers) to take action?

- What help do I need from people outside the classroom (administrators, community members, family) to take action?

Guest Speaker on Disability

Approximate time: one to two class sessions

At this point, after the participants have discussed disability, ableism, their own concerns, and their suggestions for action, we recommend that they invite a guest into the classroom to engage in a dialogue with the participants on issues of disability. We recommend that the speaker be someone who not only works on issues of disability but also has lived experience with these issues. It would be significant if the speaker were a friend or family member of one of the participants.

Local advocacy and support groups for persons with disabilities such as the ARC (formerly the Association for Retarded Citizens), United Cerebral Palsy, and United Mental Health may be able to provide or to recommend speakers.

Individual Exercise: Reading and Reflection— "Lunch Break"

Approximate time: two class sessions

Before the next class session, the participants read the poem "Lunch Break" by Laura Hershey. This poem may be read aloud in class (or signed, using American Sign Language) if participants feel that doing so would deepen their responses to it.

The participants prepare reflections on the poem in a form that displays one or more of their multiple intelligences (see Chapter 2)—an essay, a poem, a rap, a song, a dance, a drawing, an equation, a journal entry, a video, or an image. These reflections may be used in group exhibits or displays, in presentations or assemblies, or in individual portfolios.

In preparing their reflections, participants keep in mind the following questions:

QUESTIONS FOR READING AND REFLECTION

- What emotions did this reading evoke in me?
- What lived experience (mine or someone else's) did this reading make me remember?
- What did the reading tell me that I already know and think is important?
- What did the reading tell me that I didn't know and want to know more about?

In the next class sessions, participants volunteer to share their reflections. Every participant should have a chance to share his or her reflection, although not every participant may choose to do so.

Lunch Break*

Laura Hershey

Laura Hershey is a Denver, Colorado, native who describes herself as a "writer, poet, and agitator." She wrote "Lunch Break" after

---

*Laura Hershey, "Lunch Break," in Barrett Shaw (Ed.), *The Ragged Edge: The Disability Experience from the Pages of the First Fifteen Years of the Disability Rag*. Louisville, KY: Advocato Press. © 1994 Laura Hershey. Reprinted with permission.

an experience she had while attending an international women's
conference in Nairobi, Kenya.

Mid-afternoon, clouds have gone away,
as every July day, for a few hours,
in Nairobi.
Women all around:
in circles, singing
    the rich-rhythmed songs of tribes combined;
in groups, dancing
    bright clothes, muscled bodies flow;
in pairs, talking
    musical and articulate as all the voices of birds;
in solitude, listening,
    watching the rest
in wonder.

I'm with Sharon, my English friend, sharing
a sandwich and Pepsi.
We don't need to talk
as she holds the food to my mouth
and bends the straw
for my drinking;
so we listen
to the variegated chorus
of chant, question,
planning, laughter, song,
and stumbling translation
around us.

An American woman approaches me,
camera in hand.
I have seen her, these few days,
snapping the heads and faces
of African women who,
I've noticed,
often frown for their portraits.

"Mind if I take your picture?" she asks.
"Alright," I answer.
She steps back, angles
her camera from a distance, the focus
on my wheelchair—
metal frame, shortened leg rests, torn green upholstery,
large tread tires—
then she waits.
We wait too, causally posed
under the hot sun. To Sharon she says,

"Will you give her another bite?"
"No," I snap. "Get this over with."
Her face changes, as if
I had spoken the language
of the Maribou stork.

How did this happen?
Am I a curiosity
to my own countrywoman?
So be it.

I will join the gallery
of those captured in the photographer's
empty frame
and bare vision—
the Masai, Luo, Kikuyu
the Navaho, Pueblo, Sioux
the Amish
the Eskimo, the Gypsy
the children
the old, the dark, the poor
the native islander, the Oriental
and "Woman"—
not born exotic,
but made so
by collectors' frozen images.

And in these frames, these photographs
of random, nameless faces,
we all know why
so many of us are frowning.

Institutional and Cultural Ableism in the Classroom

Approximate time: two class sessions

In 1973, a survey taken by the Children's Defense Fund showed that 750,000 U.S. children were not attending school. The survey coordinator, Marian Wright Edelman, assumed that these children must be African-Americans, denied access to education by racial segregation. Edelman was surprised to discover that the 750,000 missing children were children with disabilities, shut out of schools by officials who claimed to be unable to educate them. These children included those with a variety of disabilities—mental retardation and autism; physical conditions such as muscular dystrophy, spina bifida, and paralysis that prevented them from walking up and down stairs; seizure disorders, such as epilepsy; blindness; and deafness (Shapiro, 1993).

A law passed in 1975, the Education for All Handicapped Children Act (now known as the Individuals With Disabilities Education Act), guarantees that all children have a right to an education. There are still disagreements both inside and outside the classroom about what this means. Some children with disabilities are educated in segregated schools with other students with disabilities, while others are included in the same schools—but not into the same classrooms, lunchrooms, or playground times—as students without disabilities.

Many parents of children with disabilities now advocate integrated education, in which children with disabilities share classrooms with children without disabilities. In an integrated middle school homeroom in Syracuse, New York, Joseph Shapiro (1993) observed students with autism and students without disabilities socializing and working together. "I've worked with kids who have been segregated and there's a big difference with these [integrated] kids," their teacher said. "Their behavior is much better and their intellectual level is much higher, too" (quoted in Shapiro, 1993, p. 170). Equally important, the students without disabilities in the homeroom learned to understand and empathize with their peers with disabilities.

Even in integrated classrooms, however, students with disabilities continue to struggle to participate fully in school activities. In 1990, Christine Sullivan, a California high school student who had cerebral palsy, had to sue her school to be allowed to bring her service dog, Ford, to class. In 1991, Jim Stan, a high school senior who had cancer and used a wheelchair, was barred from graduation by his principal because the principal felt that Stan's presence would disrupt the ceremony. Newspaper articles portraying the principal as coldhearted forced him to back down (Shapiro, 1993).

QUESTIONS FOR REFLECTION AND LARGE GROUP DISCUSSION

- What experiences have I had with disability and education?

- Were these experiences examples of segregated or integrated education?

- What are my school's policies and practices on the education of individuals with disabilities?

Individual Exercise: Reading and Reflection— "Giving It Back"

Approximate time: two class sessions

Before the next class session, the participants read an excerpt from the essay "Giving It Back" by Cris Matthews. This essay may be read aloud in class (or signed, using American Sign Language) if participants feel that doing so would deepen their responses to it.

The participants prepare reflections on the essay in a form that displays one or more of their multiple intelligences (see Chapter 2)—an essay, a poem, a rap, a song, a dance, a drawing, an equation, a journal entry, a video, or an image. These reflections may be used in group exhibits or displays, in presentations or assemblies, or in individual portfolios.

In preparing their reflections, participants keep in mind the following questions:

QUESTIONS FOR READING AND REFLECTION

- What emotions did this reading evoke in me?
- What lived experience (mine or someone else's) did this reading make me remember?
- What did the reading tell me that I already know and think is important?
- What did the reading tell me that I didn't know and want to know more about?

In the next class sessions, the participants volunteer to share their reflections. Every participant should have a chance to share his or her reflection, although not every participant may choose to do so.

Giving It Back*

Cris Matthews

Cris Matthews is a writer living in Chicago who also consults on accommodations and training for persons with disabilities. She describes herself as "continuing to boldly go where no crip has

---

*Cris Matthews, "Giving It Back," in Barrett Shaw (Ed.), *The Ragged Edge: The Disability Experience from the Pages of the First Fifteen Years of the Disability Rag*. Louisville, KY: Advocato Press. Copyright © 1994 Cris Matthews. Reprinted with permission.

gone before." Matthews wrote "Giving It Back" out of the anger she felt after learning of the death of her childhood friend, Gail Linn.

Two years ago Gail Linn—my best friend through most of grade school—died. Yet I found out only a week ago—accidentally.

Taking a nostalgia drive through the old neighborhood, I noticed the wheelchair ramp that had taken up most of her parents' yard was gone. I was unprepared for the news that my old friend was gone too.

We were diametric opposites, she and I. She was blonde; I have dark hair. She was shy at school, not popular; I was outgoing and had lots of friends. My parents were divorced; her family even included a live-in grandmother! She excelled at everything academic, including perfect penmanship. I was smart but struggled with math; my writing was a more "distinct" scrawl. She was five month older than me. Throughout grade school we were best friends.

Freshman year of high school meant different homerooms, different classes and even different bus routes (yes, in those days we were bused to "special" schools). Most of the friends we'd make in grade school still hung out with me; Gail Linn could be with my crowd at recess after lunch. By then I was a hippie. Gail Linn was still Gail Linn.

When I transferred to yet another gimp school, my ties to my former friend ended in the blur of adolescence and the unrelenting roll into adulthood. Through grapevines and assumptions I knew our lives had taken quite different paths. I had been on an adventure with thousands of experiences in my catalog and twice as many lessons learned. I struck out on my own and sometimes paid dearly for it, but ended up richly rewarded. I'd traveled a bit, been involved in disability civil rights confrontations in the streets of our city and was now managing to live on my own.

Gail Linn's academic brilliance brought her an offer of a full scholarship, including room, board and attendant service at a Big Ten University, at a time when gimps like us just didn't go to college. She turned it down, though, because she couldn't bear to leave home. There she stayed until she died.

When I returned to my hometown after having been away for several years, I'd once made an effort to call her, curious to see if the woman who had always had the best of everything was still on top.

We chatted, and I learned her grandmother had died, her brother moved away and sister had married—and that Donna's husband really liked Gail Linn. Poor Donna, I thought: even marriage hadn't given her an escape from her demanding older sister. Gail Linn told me that she and Donna would go to an occasional Barry Manilow concert or this or that. I saw Gail Linn was still insulated from my harsh realities.

I didn't tell her how hard it was for me to find someone to get me up in the morning. I glossed over the last broken heart I'd had; I didn't mention how I was afraid of getting old. I told her, instead, about my job. I told her I was learning to drive, and that I was now volunteering at the same summer camp that 18 years ago she'd gone home from after two days.

I realized I still knew her. I remembered the look of uncomfortable disagreement she'd wear when you knew she just didn't get it. She'd kind of shrink into herself when something seemed too much for her, in all her academic brilliance, to think about. She'd smile weakly, divert her eyes. "Oh, uh-huh," she'd say.

There wasn't much to say after that conversation. We'd hit a wall, reached an impasse even nostalgia couldn't penetrate, leaving me searching for what it had been that had held us together so long ago.

She called only once after that; I don't remember what it was we talked about. When I moved to my own place, I entertained the idea of inviting her and her parents over for dinner, to show them what people with disabilities could accomplish in these modern times. But I knew my purpose was only to gloat, so the invitation was never extended.

When I met my beloved Dave, the thought of calling Gail Linn occurred to me. But then I recalled a tearful conversation we'd once had because a neighbor boy hadn't liked her. She'd been crazy about him and he knew it. He'd told me privately once that he didn't like Gail Linn much, but that he'd come over because her mother had always been nice to his widowed mom. He'd proceeded to point out to me the things I'd thought only I noticed. He'd mocked, while I'd sat numbly, divided inside between loyalty to my defenseless friend and relief that I wasn't alone in my view of her. Through all the nights Gail Linn had weepingly prayed for Joey's conversion, I writhed in guilt, knowing the truth.

I couldn't tell her about Dave. I was afraid I'd be gloating—over finally having the one thing Gail Linn didn't.

When Gail Linn's mother told me about her daughter's death, she revealed a few things that underscored for the final time the differences that had helped us drift apart.

Gail Linn was involved in her church's young adult club. On overnight trips, her brother would go along and handle her care, because he could still lift her. The family knew nothing of attendant services—or even lifting devices that would help other women to lift her.

Her mother told me that Gail Linn, when she went down the block, would take along a cordless phone to call home in case she got in trouble. At the end of her block is an accessible bus route; Gail Linn probably never knew it existed. She would not go on her own any farther than the cordless phone would work. A beautiful city, a calm neighborhood and an accessible bus route at her door—she turned them all down. A free ticket to higher education, summer camp and access to all kinds of interesting other adventures. She couldn't cope.

I took comparatively wrong roads; traded common sense for intrigue so often it became habit. I opted for the gravel road instead of the yellow brick one. I spent so much time on self-loathing that I nearly became a burnout who could only identify friends by which barstool they sat on. My physical health and mental attitude were so poor that I almost lost my life. Much of my experience has been a voluntary boxing match. But the victory has come in a life richer than I could have predicted. Still, Gail Linn's death has made me examine my life as I've never done before.

I feel rage when I think of her life, and its lurking, stereotypic "happy cripple" motif, used as a standard for the rest of us. In school Gail Linn was demure and quiet. She followed instructions, did what she was told and never deviated from the path others presented to her. So pleased were they with her gentility! They always asked me why I couldn't "be like Gail Linn."

They didn't see the after-school side of Gail Linn. They didn't see that the instant she was lugged up the stairs to the main floor of her family home, Gail Linn became the queen of all she surveyed, using her disability to lord it over her siblings. Donna came third, even though she was the middle child (Jack, her brother, was the youngest, but his gender granted him household priorities.) Once home, Gail Linn became loud, bossy, and spoiled. The transformation was practically unbelievable.

Is the rage I feel resentment? It would have been so much easier for me had I never gone away to school, never gotten a job; if I'd never done anything more than was offered me within the two-block radius of my mother's home. The stresses of recruiting and managing attendants, paying bills or even figuring out what to eat each day could have been traded for a comfortable, predictable life with my mother. Maybe I resent Gail Linn for taking the cushy route.

Could my rage be frustration? Frustration at knowing that Gail Linn had been in a unique position for someone with a disability at that time in society—that her brain could have opened countless doors for her? Frustration knowing that she might have written her own ticket, and still ended up with a cushy life—that she had earned herself? Frustration thinking that, had she done that, she could have given something back?

She had a chance to bust a stereotype. Instead, she accepted it. That she had a life of relative ease is not what so enrages me; it's the way she accomplished it. . . .

It boils down to who controls our lives. We might think we do; but every time Jerry Lewis snivels his way across America, he takes away our control. Every time one of us decides it's easier to just take what we can take, Jerry Lewis wins. If we let people like him win, then we have no business complaining when we can't get jobs, or the services we need, or even access to the local grocery store.

It isn't up to me to decide what Gail Linn's life amounted to. But as long as I can, I will continue fighting anyone who sees our lives as pitiable—including those of us with disabilities who hold that view. I will do my best to help battle the forces that keep people like Gail Linn from doing just one little thing for someone or something outside themselves. And I will never ever again entertain the thought that I could possibly have been happy on the same road that Gail Linn chose.

A popular country song speaks to the choices we make. He could have made different, less complicated, easier choices in life, the singer croons; but he would have missed a lot in the process: "I could have lived without the pain, but I'd have had to miss the dance."

Some of us are dancers. We fly across the floor in our wheelchairs, turning them, moving them, spinning them around to the music around us. Sometimes there are patterns, sometimes it's free form. Onlookers may not consider this dancing, but it is to us. It is celebration. This is why we dance.

Some make it to the dance, then wait for someone to lead them through the steps. Few realize it's OK to invent the steps. They leave without enjoying all the dance has to offer. If someone had encouraged them from the floor, they might have danced a little, once in a while.

Others simply don't come to the dance at all, because they can't imagine how such a thing is possible. Since they can't conceive of the dance, it doesn't exist for them. They live and die without making any difference—to anyone or anything. They sat back and took all the favors, all the handouts, all good deeds done for them, without ever trying it for themselves. Whether they lived or not seemed to make no difference.

Had that song been popular when I was a kid, I might have told those so anxious for my conformity why I couldn't be like Gail Linn. "'Cause I gotta dance," I would have said. "And Gail Linn won't learn how." They couldn't have understood. But twenty-five years later, I am so glad I didn't change. What a stunningly beautiful dance I would have missed!

Gail Linn's mother summed up her daughter's life: "Well, at least all her sufferings are over." I didn't ask, but I kind of figured that she wasn't talking about the short illness at the end. My life has to be more than a testament to suffering. Existence on this earth must, in some small way, be better for my time here. Gail Linn convinced me of this. Maybe that is the meaning I've been searching her life for.

7

Continuing the Commitment

It just seems like the world is a pool of hate, and I don't think people get to know each other. . . . But I just think, if people would just get to know each other, like the inside of each other, not just what's on the outside.

I think it would be a lot.

—student from pilot program Dealing With Prejudice

To continue their commitment to dealing with differences, the participants need to remember what they have felt, thought, and done during the weeks and months of the program. They also need to carry something from the program into the future. In this chapter, participants explore what the program has meant to them and what they wish to take from it into other areas of their lives.

This chapter contains the following sections. The times given to complete them are approximate.

Icebreaker: "The Main Things" (one to two class sessions)
Reducing Prejudice (one to two class sessions)

Icebreaker: "The Main Things"

Approximate time: one to two class sessions

What are the main things that the participants want to remember from their experiences with *Dealing With Differences?* What are the main things that the participants want to continue to learn about and work on?

In the exercise "The Main Things," participants share their reflections on these questions. As with other exercises in *Dealing With Differences,* "The Main Things" depends on the participants being respectful of each other and assuming responsibility for the process.

SUPPLIES: Chalkboard and chalk or poster paper and marking pens.
STUDENT LEADERSHIP: Two or more students volunteer to help give instructions for the exercise, lead the large group discussion, and record the discussion results on the chalkboard or poster paper.
TO BEGIN: The exercise leaders ask the participants to move their desks so that there is an open space in the middle of the classroom. They then ask the participants to form a circle in the open space.

One participant begins the icebreaker by sharing the main thing he or she remembers from the program. (An example taken from the pilot program Dealing With Prejudice: "I never thought of how prejudice isn't just race, ethnicity, or gender. It comes in the form of types of clothing or looks. I never realized that I prejudged people, too. And I always thought I had an open mind.")

The person to the left of that participant speaks next. Sharing continues until everyone in the circle has spoken.

One participant then shares the main thing he or she wants to continue studying or working on. (An example taken from the pilot program Dealing With Prejudice: "I want to start a hotline for kids in trouble, staffed by teenagers.")

The person to the left of that participant speaks next. Sharing continues until everyone in the circle has spoken.

The participants return to their seats for discussion.

QUESTIONS FOR REFLECTION AND LARGE GROUP DISCUSSION

- Which "main things" remembered by other participants are important to me?

- Which "main things" that other participants want to continue studying or working on are important to me?

- What surprised me about this exercise?

Reducing Prejudice

Approximate time: one to two class sessions

Deborah Byrnes (1988) asserts that prejudice can be reduced in the classroom through four different kinds of activities:

1. Activities that promote positive interactions with those different from oneself on the basis of equality

2. Activities that promote individual self-esteem

3. Activities that encourage the identification of overgeneralizations and stereotypes

4. Activities that increase empathy for and understanding of individuals who are different from oneself

To these items, we add a fifth:

5. Activities that encourage establishment of zones of respect between oneself and others

Zones of respect are spaces where individuals can deal with their differences honestly, without using or abusing one another. These places may be physical, such as a school, church, or community center. They can be mental and emotional, such as an assembly or meeting in which individuals agree to challenge their differences without violence and with regard for one another's ideas and feelings. Zones of respect can be created among classmates, among neighbors, among family members, among friends, even among former enemies.

QUESTIONS FOR REFLECTION AND LARGE GROUP DISCUSSION

- How can I continue to engage in activities that promote positive interactions with those different from myself on the basis of equality?

- How can I continue to engage in activities that promote my individual self-esteem?

- How can I continue to engage in activities that encourage me to identify overgeneralizations and stereotypes?

- How can I continue to engage in activities that increase my empathy and understanding of individuals who are different from myself?

- How can I continue to engage in activities that encourage establishment of zones of respect between myself and others?

Small Group Exercise: Continuing the Commitment— Concerns and Suggestions for Action

Approximate time: two class sessions

What concerns raised during this program are most important to the participants? What actions can they take to address these concerns? To explore these questions, the participants assemble in the small groups formed in Chapter 2.

Action can take a variety of forms, both individual and collective. It is important that the actions students suggest—however small or incremental—are taken seriously by teachers and administrators and encouraged whenever possible. If teachers dismiss or discourage suggestions for action, students may justly complain that the program is hypocritical or irrelevant to their lives. Here are some examples of actions suggested and taken by students in the pilot program Dealing With Prejudice:

1. Speak up more for yourself and for others in the face of prejudice

2. Form an after-school discussion/action group

3. Go as a class or group to a relevant movie and discuss it afterward

4. Watch as a class or group relevant videos or TV programs

5. Read books and magazines about your concern

6. Write or call the local newspaper, radio station, or TV station about your concern

7. Boycott businesses that ignore or contribute to your concern

8. Meet as a group with school administrators about your concern

9. Volunteer with an existing school, church, or community group that works on your concern

10. Hold a student-run school assembly on your concern

11. Develop a play or presentation on your concern and perform it for the entire school

12. Develop a display or exhibit on your concern in the classroom or elsewhere on school property

SUPPLIES: Poster paper, marking pens.

STUDENT LEADERSHIP: One student in each small group volunteers to record the results of the group's discussion on poster paper.

TO BEGIN: Each small group chooses one or more concerns to explore from the list developed and recorded during previous Common Ground exercises. The group recorder then writes these four column heads on paper:

What do we know (about this concern)?

What do we need to know (about this concern)?

How can we know (about this concern)?

How can we act (on this concern)?

Using as a guideline the principles of critical thinking and I-search described in Chapter 2, each group brainstorms the concern it has chosen. Groups may consult with teachers on completing this process through trips to the school or the public library, or calls to or meetings with community members. Teachers and students decide together how much I-search can be done during the *Dealing With Differences* sessions and how much can be done outside of class.

When I-search is completed, each recorder summarizes his or her group's findings on a sheet of poster paper and posts it on the wall to be read and considered by other participants.

Large Group Exercise: Continuing the Commitment—Concerns and Suggestions for Action

Approximate time: two class sessions

In this exercise, the participants reflect on the results of the small group discussions and decide which suggestions for action they can implement as individuals, as small groups, or as a class.

SUPPLIES: Chalkboard and chalk or poster paper and marking pens.

STUDENT LEADERSHIP: Two or more students volunteer to give instructions for the exercise and to record the results of the large group discussion on the chalkboard or poster paper.

TO BEGIN: The exercise leaders ask the participants to leave their desks to read the posted results of each small group's discussion. The participants are encouraged to ask questions of one another and to make notes on what they find interesting.

After 10 to 20 minutes of mingling, the participants return to their seats for discussion.

QUESTIONS FOR REFLECTION AND LARGE GROUP DISCUSSION

- Now that I have reviewed all of the suggestions for action, what suggestions would I most like to implement?

- Are these actions I can take as an individual? As part of a group? As a member of this class?

- What help do I need from other participants (students or teachers) to take action?

- What help do I need from people outside the classroom (administrators, community members, family) to take action?

Individual Exercise: Reading and Reflection—"Lost in Emotion," "Diversity," and "Change"

Approximate time: two class sessions

Before the next class session, the participants read all three of the following writings by high school students: "Lost in Emotion," by

Jerome Clark; "Diversity," by Ayisha Amalá Morgan-Lee; and "Change," by LaNa Howard. These pieces may be read aloud in class (or signed, using American Sign Language) if participants feel that doing so would deepen their responses to the work.

The participants each prepare a reflection on one of the pieces in a form that displays one or more of their multiple intelligences (see Chapter 2)—an essay, a poem, a rap, a song, a dance, a drawing, an equation, a journal entry, a video, or an image. These reflections may be used in group exhibits or displays, in presentations or assemblies, or in individual portfolios.

In preparing their reflections, participants keep in mind the following questions:

QUESTIONS FOR READING AND REFLECTION

- What emotions did this reading evoke in me?

- What lived experience (mine or someone else's) did this reading make me remember?

- What did the reading tell me that I already know and think is important?

- What did the reading tell me that I didn't know and want to know more about?

In the next class sessions, participants volunteer to share their reflections. Every participant should have a chance to share his or her reflection, although not every participant may choose to do so.

Lost in Emotion*

Jerome Clark

Jerome Clark is high school junior who lives in Canton, Ohio. His interests include track, music, art, and fashion illustration. He wrote "Lost in Emotion" because he is concerned about the legal rights of others and the prejudices that individuals act out toward others.

I know personally how it feels to be rejected by my peers, family and the rest of society just because you choose to be different. I feel that everywhere I go people watch what I do and what I say. Dealing with the differences among us has a great deal of meaning for me. One of the most important differences to deal

---

*Jerome Clark, "Lost in Emotion." Previously unpublished paper. Copyright © 1996 Jerome Clark. Printed with permission.

with are those which separate people from one another. At times I have experienced what it is like to be separated from the people around me because of differences. Sometimes I have even chosen to separate myself from others because of differences. There are problems that occur because people can't accept each others' differences.

An example of this happened to me last year while I was a sophomore in high school. I began to hang out with a different crowd (not anyone bad or anyone who did drugs or anything like that) but a bunch of straight edges (people who do not do drugs) and vegans (non-meat-eating people) because I felt it was time to change. The kids that I used to hang with were not too down with that. One day a girl who I used to sit with at the Black table asked me to come back over to the table to talk. So I did. While we were talking two boys jumped in our convo talking mess. One of them asked me if I was straight edge. I told him I was. So, he was like, well, you know you can't eat meat. I told him I could; he threw his burger and applesauce in my face and told me not to ever correct him. I left the table and went to the bathroom and washed my face.

After lunch I had speech class with this same boy. All through speech class he called me "faggot," saying stuff like "where's your boyfriend." This really made me angry because half of my new friends were gay or bisexual which was okay with me. I felt that we were all one family. People don't know how it is to be called "gay," "homo," "lesy," or "faggot." These are words that deeply hurt people's feelings.

After the class I tried to wait him out by talking to the teacher. That didn't work because he was still waiting for me and I still had to face him. I told myself that if I walked up the steps and did not say one word nothing would happen. I heard my name being called and when I turned around I saw a couple of the guys in front of me. The same guy who had called me "faggot" in class said "You ain't talking mess now, is you?" I told him to get out of my way. Then he said, "You know I should slap you—you faggot." I said—"whatever." That's when he slapped me.

One of the teachers saw what happened and came over and broke it up. The boy got two days of in-school suspension and said he would kill me when he got out. Differences among people can really lead to a whole lot of problems, especially when they act out their prejudices.

In addition to my problem in school with my new friends, I also had problems at home. Some members of my family didn't like my friends too much. They thought they were a bunch of freaks, but they weren't. After a while they began to think that my friends' sexual preferences were influencing me, which was not true. My friends and I love each other (as brothers and sisters) and we feel that we are spiritually connected.

To this day they still do not trust my friends. My friends are not allowed to come to our house. People often wonder if I'm homosexual or bisexual—I'm not. As a matter of fact I don't even want to be termed heterosexual. I'm none of these labels. I am just a person who wants to be true to himself and to accept other people for who they are.

I live with the reality of differences and the prejudice that comes from this every day of my life. I go to school every day to get my education so I can get into college someday. But every day of my life I go to school and get tortured by other students. I have done nothing to them. Some of the kids in school still call me names like "faggot," "homo," and "freak." They call me "homo" because of who I hang out with, which is wrong.

Persons need to face their fears. My family and peers are afraid of homosexuality. Their homophobia prevents them from seeing reality. I have three cousins who are gay, and two of them have died of AIDS. This is a very sad thing and very difficult for my family to face. My family incorrectly thinks that AIDS is a homosexual disease. Because of their homophobia they can't understand that AIDS is also very common among heterosexuals.

When a gay person or a straight person comes up to you are you sure that you can know which one is which and what each one's sexual preference is? Maybe you should think about it.

At this point I will close, saying that I'm "Lost in Emotion."

Diversity*

Ayisha Amalá Morgan-Lee

Ayisha Amalá Morgan-Lee is an eighth-grade student at a grammar school in Pittsburgh, Pennsylvania. She enjoys the performing arts, computers, swimming, reading, and biking.

The first two things that come to mind to describe diversity for me is one, that diversity is a challenge and two, that diversity is a network. Diversity is a challenge because trying to bring different cultures, attitudes, styles and people together is a huge task. Diversity cannot occur as long as people are focused on their individual needs and ideas about that which is different from their normal experiences.

I have attended Duquesne University Multi-cultural Computer Academy for the past three years and that experience has not only taught me about computers but also about differences. We have had students and counselors from all over the world; they speak many languages. Some of the students are in wheelchairs; one student even has a dog that assists him in getting around. It is fun and we all learn how to work together. I always leave with a stronger understanding of others who are different from me. It is a very good positive experience. This experience has helped me to understand diversity as a network of people.

Each one of us has something to bring to the system. In the computer world, each computer in the network comes together to add something more to the information sharing and learning. Diversity allows us to come together as many different people, each unique working together as one. Connecting networks of computers together is tedious and time-consuming but when they work, the whole world opens up to you. Connecting networks of people who are diverse is challenging but when they work together, the whole world opens up to them also.

Change*

LaNa Howard

LaNa Howard is a high school junior who lives in Monroeville, Pennsylvania. She wrote "Change" after an incident in which racist literature had been circulated in her school.

We need to make a positive change in the world today.
The world today is full of hate.
Until we fill the world with love, it won't change.
Prejudice is abundant in many forms.
We must recognize each other as equals.
The world today is full of separation.
We must come together as one if we want to make change.
Many things cause destruction of self, others and our
    world.
When we learn to love destruction will stop.
When we recognize each other as equals, destruction will
    stop.
When we come together as one, destruction will stop.
When we stop destruction, we will cause a change.
Change is what we need to live in a loving,
equal world of togetherness.
But we all must start with a positive change in ourselves.
When we make a change in ourselves, love, come
    together, and
stop destruction, together we'll change the world.
And what a positive change it will be.

Closing Ceremony: "Mosaics"

Approximate time: special session, one morning or afternoon

Closing ceremonies, such as graduations, mark the end of one phase of life and the beginning of another. Ceremonies are times of remembrance, sharing, celebration, and reflection. "Mosaics" is a two-part ceremony designed to allow participants to remember, share, celebrate, and reflect on who they are and who they have become as individuals and as a group during the course of *Dealing With Differences.*

A mosaic is a pattern or picture created by putting together smaller pieces of material. Mosaics are traditionally made of hard materials such as stone, glass, or clay, but the term can be used to describe photographs or other images that resemble mosaics. Our exercise "Mosaics" was adapted from one developed by Donna Brady of the Pennsylvania Governor's School for Teaching.

PART 1

SUPPLIES (contributed by all participants): Chalkboard and chalk or poster paper and marking pens, paint, glitter, construction paper, wrapping paper, foil, cloth, beads, sticks, stones, shells, newsprint, magazines, photographs of family and friends (these must be photographs that participants are willing to cut up), scissors, tape dispensers, and bottles of glue or glue sticks.

STUDENT LEADERSHIP: Two or more students volunteer to help prepare and distribute blank mosaic triangles and to record the results of the large group discussion on the chalkboard or poster paper.

PREPARATION (done before class): The exercise leaders cut poster paper into 18-inch equilateral triangles, then fold these to create four smaller equilateral triangles, each of which will represent one aspect of a participant's self (see Figure 7.1). There should be one mosaic blank for each participant.

TO BEGIN: The teachers and exercise leaders distribute blank mosaics to the participants and place the other materials in an area for common use. Working individually or in groups, the participants create their mosaics, making sure that whatever materials they use are glued or taped securely to their blank triangles.

Each triangle within the mosaic is completed according to the following guidelines (see Figure 7.1):

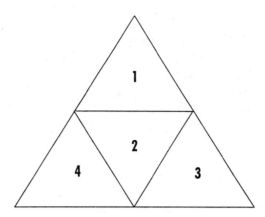

Figure 7.1. Form for Mosaic

Area 1 represents where the participant comes from—his or her place of birth, place of growing up, racial, ethnic, and religious heritages

Area 2 represents who the participant is—his or her interests, accomplishments, family, and friends

Area 3 represents what inspires the participant—whom he or she admires, what feelings and ideas are important to her or to him (quotations may be used)

Area 4 represents what the participant hopes for—what work he or she would like to accomplish, how he or she would like to help other people

When the participants have completed their mosaics, they engage in large group discussion.

QUESTIONS FOR REFLECTION AND LARGE GROUP DISCUSSION

- Which part of my mosaic did I have the hardest time completing?

- Which part of my mosaic did I have the easiest time completing?

- What do I most want other participants to know about me through my mosaic?

- What surprised me about this exercise?

PART 2

SUPPLIES: Cookies, cake, soft drinks, punch; camera or video recorder.

TO BEGIN: The participants move their mosaics to the school cafeteria and lay them out on a table or tables for individual display. They take a few minutes to admire the mosaics as individual pieces. The exercise leaders may take photographs of or videotape the mosaics.

The participants then rearrange the mosaics in a pattern, so that the edges are touching. This pattern is determined by each participant joining his or her mosaic to the sides of other mosaics that are *similar* to his or hers in some way—background, interests, inspirations, hopes. Every mosaic should touch at least one other mosaic.

Each participant then says at least one sentence about why and where he or she chose to place a mosaic. The exercise leaders may take photographs of or videotape the pattern.

The participants then rearrange the mosaics in another pattern, created by each participant joining his or her mosaic to the sides of other mosaics that are *different* from his or hers in some way—background, interests, inspirations, hopes. Every mosaic should touch at least one other mosaic.

Each participant then says at least one sentence about why and where he or she chose to place a mosaic. The exercise leaders may take photographs or videotape the pattern.

The participants chat and share refreshments. The exercise leaders may take photographs of or videotape (including mini-interviews with participants) of this part of the closing ceremony.

The participants may decide later to set up a display of their mosaics in their school or their community. Photographs, videos, and student reflections, as well as the mosaics themselves, can be used in this display.

Afterword

Dealing With Differences challenges educators to explore the differences and connections of race, gender, class, and disability in ways that allow students to understand the multifaceted dynamics of diversity. In *Dealing With Differences,* students are viewed as critical thinkers capable of and responsible for creating change through action in their own lives and in the broader community. *Dealing With Differences* challenges teachers and students to see differences in ways that foster new awareness and understanding of self and others.

As an educator, I have always viewed diversity as both our greatest gift and our greatest challenge. Educators have the task of engaging students in learning processes that will allow them to see the richness of diversity with new eyes and to hear the richness of diversity with new ears. Teachers who adopt *Dealing With Differences* are initiating a very important step in the educational change process of their students.

The question then becomes, How can this momentum be sustained with students? What new endeavors can be initiated as a result of the insights and sensitivities gained through the use of *Dealing With Differences?* What can teachers and students do to continue conversations that were socially urgent and personally transforming?

Dealing With Differences offers many opportunities to expand students' personal knowledge of differences. Throughout the program, students are asked to explore their images of race, gender, class, and disability. These images are further explored in discussions of language and the ways in which words are used to define differences and perpetuate prejudices. Building on these experiences,

ences, students can be challenged to explore new experiences with those who are different from themselves. Prejudices begin to break down when individuals experience that which is different and expand their knowledge and understanding of differences.

Teachers could involve students in experiences with persons who are racially, ethnically, and physically different, such as a partner or buddy relationship. The buddy relationship should be one where students are challenged to learn through the eyes of another person for a sufficient amount of time to allow the development of meaningful relationships.

The commitment to diversity is a challenging one. It continually reshapes our questions, our definitions, and our values. Teachers and students who have experienced *Dealing With Differences* are challenged to respond in new and different ways to issues of race, gender, class, and disability. Teachers can enable students to see their school and communities differently. Class assignments that encourage students to address ways to encourage more equitable interactions with groups that are seen as different could provide students with opportunities to construct a new societal order in the school and in their communities. Students should be encouraged to use their new understandings about differences to restructure their interactions with others, both in case models and in volunteer experiences that focus on opportunities for change.

The mosaic exercise in Chapter 7 could inspire teachers to engage a homeroom or a classroom by commissioning a mosaic of differences, weaving a rich tapestry of diversity of people by race, gender, class, and ability. This mosaic could give students the opportunity to work together, respecting their differences of learning, academic abilities, and artistic abilities as well as their differences of race, gender, class, and physical and mental abilities. It could open students to new challenges, because while constructing this mosaic, they would do research and conduct oral interviews in areas they had not previously explored. This mosaic could be commissioned at the beginning of a term and completed at the end of the term, giving students months to immerse themselves in the project. The mosaic of differences could be a total school project or a class project, that is, of seniors, juniors, or some other grouping of students.

The future activities that I have outlined have students and teachers engaging in actions that take them out of their world into the world of others. This focus involves risk; yet when done with sincerity, it can provide students with lasting and often haunting memories of transformative experiences during their journeys to learn more about and be more sensitive to differences. Teachers also can use traditional methods of engaging students, such as topical essays and class dialogues, in their further study of differences.

Dealing With Differences is a book that challenges teachers, students, and the school community to see differences not as issues or problems but rather as opportunities to share differences in ways that affirm and value the diversity of race, gender, class, and ability. It provides students with opportunities to search and question the origins of their prejudices about race, gender, class, and ability. It empowers teachers and students to become engaged as learners in a commitment to diversity.

Dealing With Differences continually reshapes the questions, definitions and visions of the learning community, moving students and teachers to transforming experiences. It is important that these experiences be connected back to the program and that teachers and students assess what changes have occurred and are occurring as a result of *Dealing With Differences*.

Veronica Morgan-Lee, Ph.D.
Director of Carlow Hill College
Carlow College
Pittsburgh, Pennsylvania

References

Allport, G. (1979). *The nature of prejudice* (25th anniversary ed.). New York: Addison-Wesley. (Original work published 1954)

American Association of University Women. (1991). *Shortchanging girls, shortchanging America: A call to action.* Washington, DC: Author.

Armstrong, T. (1994). *Multiple intelligences in the classroom.* Alexandria, VA: ASCD.

Baca, J. S. (1982). *What's happening.* Willimantic, CT: Curbstone Press.

Barndt, J. (1991). *Dismantling racism: The continuing challenge to white America.* Minneapolis, MN: Augsburg Fortress.

Barlett, D., & Steele, J. B. (1992). *America: What went wrong?* Kansas City, MO: Andrews & McMeel.

Bell, D. (1992). *Faces at the bottom of the well: The permanence of racism.* New York: Basic Books.

Brown, L. M., & Gilligan, C. (1992). *Meeting at the crossroads: Women's psychology and girls' development.* New York: Ballantine.

Byrnes, D. (1988, April/May). Children and prejudice. *Social Education,* pp. 267-271.

Christian-Smith, L. K. (1993). Voices of resistance: Young women readers of romance fiction. In L. Weis & M. Fine (Eds.), *Beyond silenced voices* (pp. 169-190). Albany: State University of New York Press.

Creighton, A., & Kivel, P. (1992). *Helping teens stop violence: A practical guide for educators, counselors, and parents* (2nd ed.). Alameda, CA: Hunter House.

D'Angelo, E. (1971). *The teaching of critical thinking.* Amsterdam, The Netherlands: B. R. Gruner.

Dolbeare, K., & Hubbell, J. K. (1996). *U.S.A. 2012: After the middle-class revolution.* Chatham, NJ: Chatham House.

Education for All Handicapped Children Act of 1975, 20 U.S.C. § 1400 *et seq.*

Eilers, F. (1993). *Communicating between cultures: An introduction to intercultural communication.* Indore, India: Satprakashan Sanchar Kendra.

Farley, R. (1993). The common destiny of blacks and whites: Observations about the social and economic status of the races. In H. Hill & J. E. Jones, Jr. (Eds.), *Race in America: The struggle for equality* (pp. 197-233). Madison: University of Wisconsin Press.

Fine, M. (1995). *Habits of mind: Struggling over values in America's classrooms.* San Francisco: Jossey-Bass.

Freeman, G. S., & Freeman, R. S. (1962). *Yesterday's toys: One of a series on bygone Americana.* Watkins Glen, NY: Century House.

Fricke, A. (1981). *Reflections of a rock lobster: A story about growing up gay.* Boston: Alyson.

Friend, R. A. (1987). The individual and social psychology of aging: Clinical implications for lesbians and gay men. *Journal of Homosexuality, 14*(1/2) 307-331.

Friend, R. A. (1993). Choices, not closets: Heterosexism and homophobia in schools. In L. Weis & M. Fine (Eds.), *Beyond silenced voices* (pp. 209-236). Albany: State University of New York Press.

Gardner, H. (1993). *Multiple intelligences: The theory in practice.* New York: Basic Books.

Gay, K. (1995). *"I am who I am": Speaking out about multiracial identity.* New York: Franklin Watts.

Hacker, A. (1992). *Two nations: Black and white, separate, hostile, and unequal.* New York: Scribners.

Harris, L., & Associates. (1994). *Hostile hallways: The AAUW survey on sexual harassment in America's schools.* Washington, DC: American Association of University Women.

Hershey, L. (1994). Lunch break. In B. Shaw (Ed.), *The ragged edge: The disability experience from the pages of the first fifteen years of the* Disability Rag. Louisville, KY: Advocato.

hooks, b. (1984). *Feminism from margin to center.* Boston: South End.

hooks, b. (1994). *Outlaw culture: Resisting representations.* New York: Routledge.

Howe, C. (1992). *Political ideology and class formation: A study of the middle class.* Westport, CT: Praeger.

Howard, L. (1995). *The tapestry.* Monroeville, PA: Gateway High School.

Kaiser, S. (1990). *The social psychology of clothing: Symbolic appearances in context* (2nd ed.). New York: Macmillan.

Kaplan, J. (Ed.). (1992). *Bartlett's familiar quotations* (16th ed.). Boston: Little, Brown.

Kleg, M. (1993). *Hate, prejudice, and racism.* Albany: State University of New York Press.

Kraut, A. M. (1994). *Silent travelers: Germs, genes, and the "immigrant menace."* New York: Basic Books.

Longmore, P. (1995, September/October). The second phase: From disability rights to disability culture. *The Disability Rag & Resource,* pp. 4-11.

Mathews, L. (1996, July 6). More than identity rides on a new racial category. *New York Times,* pp. 1, 7.

McRobbie, A. (1978). Working class girls and the culture of femininity. In Women's Studies Group (Ed.), *Women take issue*. London: Hutchinson.

Meier, D. (1995). *The power of their ideas: Lessons for America from a small school in Harlem*. Boston: Beacon.

Mickelson, R. A., Smith, S. S., & Oliver, M. L. (1993). Breaking through the barriers: African American job candidates and the academic hiring process. In L. Weis & M. Fine (Eds.), *Beyond silenced voices* (pp. 9-24). Albany: State University of New York Press.

Mishel, L., & Bernstein, J. (1994). *The state of working America* (EPI Study Series). Armonk, NY: M. E. Sharpe.

Morgan-Lee, A. A. (1996). *Diversity*. Unpublished manuscript.

Nackenoff, C. (1994). *The fictional Republic: Horatio Alger and American political discourse*. New York: Oxford University Press.

New shorter Oxford English dictionary. (1993). (L. Brown, Ed.). New York: Oxford University Press.

Newman, K. (1996, July 25/August 5). Working poor, working hard. *The Nation*, pp. 20-23.

Oakes, J. (1985). *Keeping track: How schools structure inequality*. New Haven, CT: Yale University Press.

Ohio State Department of Education. (1985). *Citizenship, multicultural and human relations education* (Minimum Standards Leadership Series, Writing Team Chair, Frank Schiraldi).

Orenstein, P. (1994). *Schoolgirls: Young women, self-esteem, and the confidence gap*. Garden City: Doubleday.

Rothenberg, P. (1992). Construction, deconstruction, and reconstruction of difference. In R. M. Baird & S. E. Rosenbaum (Eds.), *Bigotry, prejudice and hatred: Definitions, causes and solutions* (pp. 47-64). Buffalo, NY: Prometheus.

Sadker, M., & Sadker, D. (1994). *Failing at fairness: How our schools cheat girls*. New York: Simon & Schuster.

Shapiro, J. (1993). *No pity: People with disabilities forging a new civil rights movement*. New York: Times Books.

Shor, I. (1992). *Empowering education: Critical teaching for social change*. Chicago: University of Chicago Press.

Sleeter, C. E., & Grant, C. A. (1987). An analysis of multicultural education in the United States. *Harvard Educational Review, 7*, 421-444.

Stevenson, R. B., & Ellsworth, J. (1993). Dropouts and the silencing of critical voices. In L. Weis & M. Fine (Eds.), *Beyond silenced voices* (pp. 259-271). Albany: State University of New York Press.

Taylor, O. (1987). *Cross cultural communication: An essential dimension of effective education*. Washington, DC: Mid-Atlantic Center for Race Equity.

United for a Fair Economy. (1995). [Training materials]. (Distributed by Share the Wealth, 37 Temple Place, 3rd floor, Boston, MA 0211.)

U.S. Bureau of the Census. (1995). *Current population report P-60*. Washington, DC: U.S. Department of Commerce.

U.S. Department of Labor, Bureau of Labor Statistics. (1995). *Employment and earnings* (Vol. 42, No. 1). Washington, DC: Author.

Valli, L. (1986). *Becoming clerical workers*. Boston: Routledge & Kegan Paul.

Wade, C. M. (1994). Disability culture rap. In B. Shaw (Ed.), *The ragged edge: The disability experience from the pages of the first fifteen years of the* Disability Rag (pp. 15-18). Louisville, KY: Advocato.

Weis, L. (1993). White male working class youth: An exploration of relative privilege and loss. In L. Weis & M. Fine (Eds.), *Beyond silenced voices* (pp. 237-258). Albany: State University of New York Press.

Wolf, N. (1992). *The beauty myth: How images of beauty are used against women.* Garden City: Anchor/Doubleday.

Wolfe, K. (1994). Springtime for Hitler. In B. Shaw (Ed.), *The ragged edge: The disability experience from the pages of the first fifteen years of the* Disability Rag (pp. 212-217). Louisville, KY: Advocato.

Resource List

The following is a selected resource list of books, periodicals, videos, and organizations intended to supplement the exercises, discussion topics, and readings in the body of *Dealing With Differences*. Sources for all films and videos are included at the end of this list.

Teaching and Learning

BOOKS AND PERIODICALS

Delpit, L. (1995). *Other people's children: Cultural conflict in the classroom.* New York: The New Press.

Democracy and Education, College of Education, 210 McCracken Hall, Ohio University, Athens, OH 45701. (614) 593-4531. $20/year (quarterly).

Education and Urban Society, Corwin Press, P.O. 2455 Teller Rd., Thousand Oaks, CA 91320. FAX: (805) 499-0871.

Horton, M., Kohl, J., & Kohl, H. (1990). *The long haul: An autobiography.* Garden City: Anchor.

King, L. (Ed.). (1991). *Hear my voice: A multicultural anthology of literature from the United States.* Menlo Park, CA: Addison-Wesley.

Levine, D., Lowe, R., Peterson, B., & Tenorio, R. (Eds.). (1995). *Rethinking schools: An agenda for change.* New York: The New Press.

Multicultural Review, Greenwood Publishing Group, 88 Post Road West, Box 5007, Westport, CT 06881-5007. (203) 226-3571. $59/year (quarterly).

New Youth Connections, 144 W. 27th Street, 8R, New York 10001. (212) 242-3270. $10/year (7 issues).

Nieto, S. (1992). *Affirming diversity: The sociopolitical context of multicultural education.* New York: Longman.

151

Pignatelli, F., & Pflaum, S. W. (Eds.). (1992). *Celebrating diverse voices: Progressive education and equity.* Newbury Park, CA: Corwin Press.

Race, Gender, and Class, Institute for Teaching and Research on Women, Towson State University, Towson, MD 21204-7097. (410) 830-2580. FAX: (410) 830-3469. E-mail: e7a8bel@toe.towson

Radical Teacher Magazine, Boston Women's Teachers' Group, P.O. Box 102, Kendall Square Post Office, Cambridge, MA 02142. $10/year for individuals, $16/year for organizations (3 issues).

Rethinking Schools, 1001 E. Keefe Avenue, Milwaukee, WI 53212. (414) 964-9646. $12.50/year (quarterly).

Shor, I., & Freire, P. (1987). *A pedagogy for liberation: Dialogue on transforming education.* Granby, MA: Bergin & Garvey.

Takaki, R. A. (1993). *A different mirror.* Boston: Little, Brown.

Teaching and Change, Corwin Press, 2455 Teller Road, Thousand Oaks, CA 91320. (805) 499-9774. FAX: (805) 499-0871.

Urban Education, Corwin Press, 2455 Teller Road, Thousand Oaks, CA 91320. (805) 499-9774. FAX: (805) 449-0871.

Z Magazine, 18 Millfield Street, Woods Hole, MA 02543. $26/year (11 issues).

Zinn, H. (1980). *A people's history of the United States.* New York: Harper & Row.

ORGANIZATIONS

Center for Collaborative Education, 1573 Madison Avenue, Room 201, New York, NY 10029. (212) 348-7821.

Coalition for Essential Schools, Box 1969, Brown University, Providence, RI 02912.

National Coalition of Education Activists (NCEA), P.O. Box 679, Rhinebeck, NY 12572-0679. (914) 876-4580.

Network of Educators on the Americas, P.O. Box 73038, Washington, DC 20056. (202) 806-7277.

Study Circles Resource Center, 697A Pomfret Street, P.O. Box 203, Pomfret, CT 06258. (203) 928-2616.

Class

FILMS AND VIDEOS

The Killing Floor - 118 min. (New Day Films)
Matewan - 100 min. (New Day Films)
Miles of Smiles, Years of Struggle - 58 min. (California Newsreel)
Union Maids - 55 min. (New Day Films)

BOOKS AND PERIODICALS

American Social History Project. (1992). *Who built America?* (2 vols.). New York: Pantheon.

Barlett, D., & Steele, J. (1994). *America: Who really pays the taxes?* New York: Simon & Schuster.

Brouwer, S. (1992). *Sharing the pie: A disturbing picture of the U.S. economy.* Carlisle, PA: Big Picture Books.

Dermott, B. (1990). *The imperial middle: Why Americans can't think straight about class.* New York: William Morrow.

Dollars and Sense, One Summer Street, Somerville, MA 02143. (617) 628-8411. $18.95/year (6 issues).

Galbraith, J. K. (1992). *The culture of contentment.* New York: Houghton Mifflin.

Geoghegan, T. (1991). *Which side are you on? Trying to be for labor when it's flat on its back.* New York: Farrar, Straus & Giroux.

Greider, W. (1992). *Who will tell the people: The betrayal of American democracy.* New York: Simon & Schuster.

New Internationalist, 1011 Bloor Street West, Suite 300, Toronto, Ontario, M6H 1M1. (416) 588-6478. $34/year (monthly).

Peterson, W. (1994). *Silent depression: The fate of the American dream.* New York: Norton.

Phillips, K. (1990). *The politics of rich and poor: Wealth and the American electorate in the Reagan aftermath.* New York: HarperCollins.

Phillips, K. (1993). *Boiling point: Democrats, Republicans, and the decline of middle-class prosperity.* New York: Random House.

Wolff, E. (1995). *Top heavy: A study of the increasing inequality of wealth in America.* New York: The Twentieth Century Fund Press.

ORGANIZATIONS

Citizen Budget Campaign of Western Pennsylvania, Thomas Merton Center, 5125 Penn Avenue, Pittsburgh, PA 15224. (412) 361-3022. FAX: (412) 361-0540.

Common Agenda Coalition, 424 C Street, NE, Washington, DC 20002. (202) 544-8222. FAX: (202) 544-8226.

Food First, 398 60th Street, Oakland, CA 94618. (510) 654-4400.

National Priorities Project, Inc., 160 Main Street, Suite #6, Northampton, MA 01060. (413) 584-9556. FAX: (413) 586-9647.

Share the Wealth, A Project of United for a Fair Economy, 37 Temple Place, Fifth Floor, Boston, MA 02111. (617) 423-2148. FAX: (617) 695-1295, E-mail: STW@STW.ORG Internet: http://www.stw.org/stw

Tax the Rich, P.O. Box 8090, Middletown, CT 06457. Internet: http://www.webcom.com/~trr

U.S. Committee for UNICEF, Education Department, 333 E. 38th Street., New York, NY 10016. (212) 922-2510.

War Resisters League, 339 Lafayette Street, New York, NY 10012. (212) 228-0450. FAX: (212) 228-6193. E-mail: wrl@igc.apc.org

Women's International League for Peace and Freedom, 1213 Race Street, Philadelphia, PA 19107. (215) 563-7110. FAX: (215) 563-5527. E-mail: wilpfnatl@igc.apc.org

Race

FILMS AND VIDEOS

The Arab World - 2 hrs. 20 min. [5 cassettes] (Wellpring Media)
At the River I Stand - 56 min. (California Newsreel)
Beyond Hate - 120 min. (ADL Materials Library)
Black Is Black Ain't - 87 min. (California Newsreel)

Color Adjustment - 88 min. (California Newsreel)
Crimes of Hate - 27 min. (ADL Materials Library)
Ethnic Notions - 56 min. (California Newsreel)
Eyes on the Prize - series. 60 min. each. (PBS Video)
Foreign Talk - 11 min. (ADL Materials Library for Heaven Lee Productions)
Frosh - 98 min. (California Newsreel)
Goin' to Chicago - 71 min. (California Newsreel)
Jews and Americans - 30 min. (Cine Research Association)
Just Black? Multi-Racial Identity - 57 min. (Filmmakers Library)
Ku Klux Klan: The Invisible Empire - 45 min. (ADL Materials Library)
Native American Studies on Video - series (Films for the Humanities and Sciences)
The Politics of Love—In Black and White - 33 min. (California Newsreel)
A Question of Color - 33 min. (California Newsreel)
The Road to Brown - 56 min. (California Newsreel)
Skin Deep - 53 min. (California Newsreel)
Surviving Columbus: The Story of the Pueblo People -120 min. (Wellspring Media)
Trouble Behind - 56 min. (California Newsreel)
We Shall Overcome - 60 min. (California Newsreel & select video stores)
Yellow Tale Blues: Two American Families - 30 min. (Filmmakers Library)

BOOKS AND PERIODICALS

Banks, J. A. (1991). *Teaching strategies for ethnic studies* (5th ed.). Boston: Allyn & Bacon.

Chan, J. P., Chin, F., Inoda, L. F., & Wong, S. (Eds.). (1991). *The big aiiee! An anthology of Chinese American and Japanese American literature.* New York: Meridian.

hooks, b. (1989). *Talking back: Thinking feminist, thinking black.* Boston: South End.

Interrace, P.O. Box 15566, Beverly Hills, CA 90209. $24/year (monthly).

Journal of American Indian Educator, Center for Indian Education, College of Education, Arizona State University, Tempe, AZ 85287. $16/year (3 issues).

Magill, F. (Ed.). (1992). *Masterpieces of African American literature.* New York: HarperCollins.

Multicultural Education, Caddo Gap Press, 3145 Geary Boulevard, Suite 275, San Francisco, CA 94118. (415) 750-9978.

Strom, M. S., & Parsons, W. (1982). *Facing history and ourselves: Holocaust and human behavior.* Watertown, MA: Intentional Educations.

Teaching Tolerance, 400 Washington Avenue, Montgomery, AL 36104. Free (twice yearly).

ORGANIZATIONS

Anti-Defamation League (ADL), 823 United Nations Plaza, New York, NY 10017. (800) 343-5540.

The Common Destiny Alliance (CODA), Benjamin Bldg. Rm. 4114, University of Maryland, College Park, MD 20742-1121. (301) 405-2341.

Facing History and Ourselves, 16 Hurd Road, Brookline, MA 02146. (617) 232-0281.

International Pen Friends, c/o Leslie Fox, P.O. Box 290065, Brooklyn, NY 11229.

National Association for Multicultural Education (NAME), 2101-A North Rolfe Street, Arlington, VA 22209-1007. (703) 243-4525.

National MultiCultural Institute (NMCI), 3000 Connecticut Avenue NW, Suite 438, Washington, DC 20008. (202) 483-0700. FAX: (202) 483-5233.

Southern Poverty Law Center, 400 Washington Avenue, Montgomery, AL 36104.

Gender

FILMS AND VIDEOS

Defending Our Lives - 30 min. (Cambridge Documentary Films)
Killing Us Softly - 30 min., and the updated version *Still Killing Us Softly* - 32 min. (Cambridge Documentary Films)
School's Out: Lesbian and Gay Youth - 30 min. (Cinema Guild)
Sticks, Stones, and Stereotypes - 26 min. (Equity Institute, Inc.)
The Times of Harvey Milk - 90 min. (October Films)

BOOKS AND PERIODICALS

Bass, E., & Kaufman, K. (1996). *Free your mind: The book for gay, lesbian, and bisexual youth—and their allies.* New York: HarperPerennial.

Brown, R. M. (1988). *Rubyfruit jungle.* New York: Bantam. (Original work published 1973)

Due, L. (1995). *Joining the tribe: Growing up gay & lesbian in the 90s.* Garden City: Anchor.

Fishman, S. B. (Ed.). (1992). *Follow my footprints: Changing images of women in American Jewish fiction.* Hanover, NH: University Press of New England.

Heron, A. (Ed.). (1994). *Two teenagers in twenty: Writings by gay and lesbian youth.* Boston: Alyson.

hooks, b. (1993). *Sisters of the yam: Black women and self-recovery.* Boston: South End.

Jennings, K. (Ed.). (1994). *Becoming visible: A reader in gay and lesbian history for high school and college students.* Boston: Alyson.

Lorde, A. (1984). *Sister outsider: Essays and speeches.* New York: Crossing.

Remafedi, G. (1994). *Death by denial: Studies of suicide in gay and lesbian teenagers.* Boston: Alyson.

Singer, B. L. (Ed.). (1994). *Growing up gay/growing up lesbian: A literary anthology.* New York: New Press.

Unks, G. (Ed.). (1995). *The gay teen: Educational practice and theory for lesbian, gay, and bisexual adolescents.* New York: Routledge.

ORGANIZATIONS

Boston Alliance of Gay, Lesbian, Bisexual, Transgender, and Questioning Youth (BAGLY), Box 814, Boston, MA 02103. (800) 422-2459. TTY: (617) 983-9845. Internet: http://www.bagly.org/bagly

Campaign to End Homophobia, Box 438316, Chicago, IL 60643-8316. (617) 868-8280.

Gay, Lesbian, and Straight Teachers Network (GLSTN), 122 West 26th Street, Suite 1100, New York, NY 10001. (212) 727-0254. E-mail: glstn@glstn.org Internet: http://www.glstn.org/freedom

Harvard Gay and Lesbian School Issues Project, Harvard Graduate School of Education, 2 Appian Way, 10 Longfellow Hall, Cambridge, MA 02138. (617) 491-5301. E-mail: lipkinar@hugse1.harvard.edu

HealthWorks Theater, 3171 North Halsted Street, 2nd Floor, Chicago, IL 60657-4435. (312) 929-4260. FAX: (312) 404-6815. E-mail: hwt96@aol.com

Horizons Community Services, 961 West Montana, Chicago, IL 60614. (312) 472-6469. FAX: (312) 472-6643. HELPLINE: (312) 327-4357.

Indiana Youth Group (IYG), Box 20716, Indianapolis, IN 46220. (317) 541-8726. FAX: (317) 545-8594. HELPLINE: (800) 347-TEEN.

National Advocacy Coalition on Youth and Sexual Orientation, 1025 Vermont Avenue, Suite 200, Washington, DC 20005. (202) 783-4165. FAX: (202) 347-2263.

National Institute for Gay, Lesbian, Bisexual and Transgender Concerns in Education, Inc., Box 249, Malden, MA 02148. (617) 321-3569. FAX: (617) 321-9901.

National Resource Center for Youth Services, 202 West Eighth Street, Tulsa, OK 74119-1419. (918) 585-2986. FAX: (918) 592-1841.

National Women's History Project, 7738 Bell Road, Windsor, CA 95492. (707) 838-6000.

The P.E.R.S.O.N. Project, 586 62nd Street, Oakland, CA 94609-1245, (510) 601-8883. FAX: (510) 601-8883. Email: jessea@uclink2. berkeley.edu

Project 21, Gay and Lesbian Alliance Against Defamation/San Francisco Bay Area, 514 Castro Street, Suite B, San Francisco, CA 94114. (415) 861-4588.

Women and Earth Global Eco-Network, 467 Central Park West, Suite 7F, New York, NY 10025. (212) 866-8130. FAX: (516) 368-1652. E-mail: womearth@dorsal.org Internet: http//www.dorsal.org/ womearth

Women's Educational Equity Act (WEEA) Publishing Center, Education Development Center, Inc., 55 Chappel Street, Suite 200, Newton, MA 02160.

Women's Educational Media, 2180 Bryant Street #203, San Francisco, CA 94110. (415) 641-4616. FAX: (415) 641-4632.

Disability

FILMS AND VIDEOS

Breaking the Silence Barrier - 30 min. (Indiana University)
Educating Peter - 30 min. (Program Development Associates)
Nobody's Burning Wheelchairs - 15 min. (National Easter Seals Society)
Small Differences - 20 min. (United Cerebral Palsy Association of Pittsburgh)
Tell Them I'm a Mermaid - 30 min. (Films Incorporated)

BOOKS AND PERIODICALS

Condeluci, A. (1995). *Interdependence: The route to community.* Winter Park, FL: GR Press.

Dickenson, M. (1987). *Thumbs up: The life and courageous comeback of White House press secretary, Jim Brady.* New York: William Morrow.

Driedger, D., & Gray, S. (Eds.). (1992). *Imprinting our image: An international anthology by women with disabilities.* Charlottetown, PEI, Canada: Gynergy Books.

Gallagher, H. G. (1985). *FDR's splendid deception.* New York: Dodd, Mead.

Grandin, T., & Scariano, M. (1986). *Emergence: Labeled autistic.* Novato, CA: Arena.

Groce, N. E. (1985). *Everyone here spoke sign language: Hereditary deafness on Martha's Vineyard.* Cambridge, MA: Harvard University Press.

Hershey, L. [Poetry, books, and tapes]. P.O. Box 9004, Denver, CO 80209.

Hockenberry, J. (1995). *Moving violations: War zones, wheelchairs, and declarations of independence.* New York: Hyperion.

Kaysen, S. (1993). *Girl, interrupted.* New York: Turtle Bay.

Stewart, J. (1989). *The body's memory.* New York: St. Martin's.

ORGANIZATIONS

The Arc (formerly the Association for Retarded Citizens). (800) 433-5255.

National Easter Seals Society, 70 East Lake Street, Chicago, IL 60601. (312) 726-6200.

National Federation for the Blind, 1800 Johnson Street, Baltimore, MD 21230. (410) 659-9314.

National Mental Health Association, 1021 Prince Street, Alexandria, VA 22314-2971. (703) 684-7722.

National Multiple Sclerosis Society, 733 3rd Avenue, New York, NY 10017-3288. (800) 344-4867.

United Cerebral Palsy Association, 14190 First Avenue NE, Shoreline, WA 98155. (206) 363-7303.

Sources for Films and Videos

ADL (Anti-Defamation League) Materials Library, 22-D Hollywood Avenue, Ho-Ho-Kus, NJ 07423. (800) 343-5540. FAX: (201) 652-1973. E-mail: tmcndy@aol.com

California Newsreel, 149 Ninth Street, Suite 420, San Francisco, CA 94103. (415) 621-6196. FAX: (415) 621-6522. Voice mail: (415) 621-6196. E-mail: newsreel@ix.netcom.com

Cambridge Documentary Films, P.O. Box 385, Cambridge, MA 02139. (617) 484-3993.

Cine Research Association, 170 Garden Street, Cambridge, MA 02139. (617) 442-9756.

Cinema Guild, Inc., 1697 Broadway, Suite 506, New York, NY 10019-5904. (800) 723-5522. FAX: (212) 246-5525.

Equity Institute, 6400 Hollis Street, Emeryville, CA 94608. (510) 658-4577.

Filmmakers Library, 124 E. 40th Street, Suite 901, New York, NY 10016.

Films Incorporated, 5547 North Raisinswood Avenue, Chicago, IL 60640. (312) 878-7300.

Films for the Humanities and Sciences, P.O. Box 2053, Princeton, NJ 08543-2053. (800) 257-5126.

Indiana University, Instructional Support Service, Franklin Hall, Bloomington, IN 47405. (812) 855-2103.

National Easter Seals Society, 70 East Lake Street, Chicago, IL 60601. (312) 726-6200.

New Day Films. (212) 967-6899.

October Films, Attn: Linda Duchin, 45 Rockefeller Plaza, Suite 304, New York, NY 10111. (212) 332-2480.

Program Development Associates, 5620 Business Avenue, Suite B, Cicero, NY 13039. (315) 452-0643.

PBS Video. (800) 328-7271.

United Cerebral Palsy Association of Pittsburgh, 4638 Centre Avenue, Pittsburgh, PA 15213. (412) 683-7100.

Wellspring Media, 65 Bleecker Street, 5th floor, New York, NY 10012. (800) 538-5856.